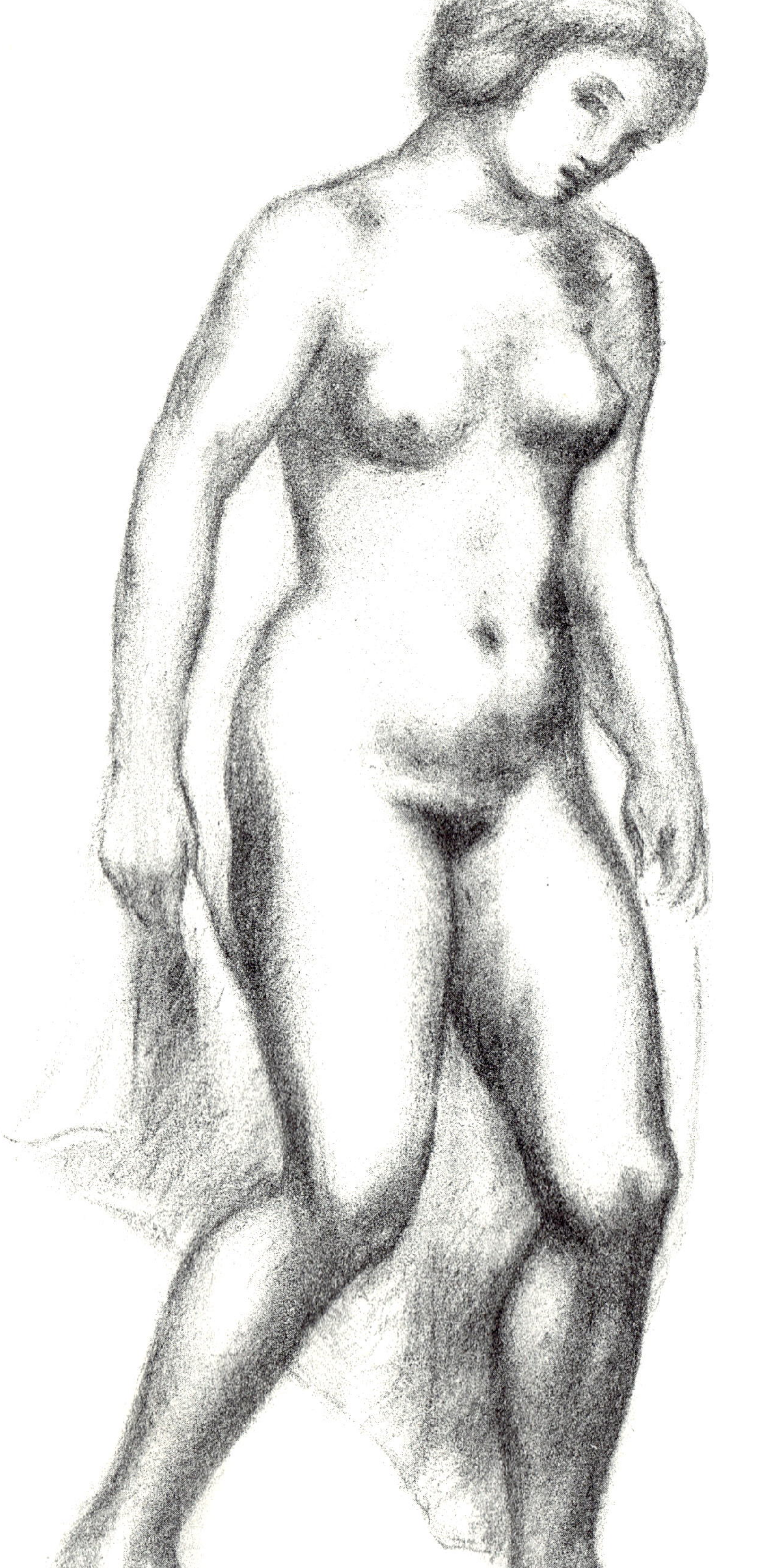

MAILLOL NUDES

35 Lithographs by

Aristide Maillol

Dover Publications, Inc., New York

PUBLISHER'S NOTE

The great modern artist Aristide Maillol (1861–1944) is best known for his exuberant sculptures celebrating the women of his native region, the Mediterranean coast of France just north of Spain. Yet Maillol was also an extremely important printmaker and book illustrator. With particular affinities to the world of ancient Greece and Rome, he illustrated such authors as Vergil, Horace, Ovid, Longus and Lucian. In all these works, as in his statues, he continued to glorify the female form.

The present volume includes all 35 of the lithographs (only seven are somewhat smaller than original size) that Maillol prepared for a French-language edition of *The Dialogues of the Courtesans (Hetairikoi Dialogoi),* written by the Greek comic author Lucian of Samosata in the second century A.D. Part of Lucian's famous series of satirical dialogues, these short witty pieces deal with the everyday doings and concerns of professional "kept women": dropping a penniless lover in favor of a rich one; preventing the marriage of a lover to preserve that source of income; and the like.

For Maillol the text in this case was only a springboard for the creation of magnificent nudes. Whereas most of his book illustrations were executed in the medium of woodcut, these rich works of the artist's mature years are lithographs. The great freedom of rendering made possible by the lithographic crayon allows each nuance of line and tone to receive its full expression.

Maillol Nudes: 35 Lithographs by Aristide Maillol, first published by Dover Publications, Inc., in 1980, contains all the illustrations from *Lucien: Dialogues des courtisanes,* printed by Pierre Bricage, Paris, in an edition of 275 copies, in 1948 (no publisher's name expressed; the edition was "réalisée" [conceived and produced] by Henri Creuzevault and Dina Vierny).

The Publisher's Note was written specially for the present edition.

The publisher is most grateful to the private collector in New York who made this rare copy of the original publication available for direct offset photography.

International Standard Book Number: 0-486-24000-2
Library of Congress Catalog Card Number: 80-65451

Manufactured in the United States of America
Dover Publications, Inc.
180 Varick Street
New York, N.Y. 10014

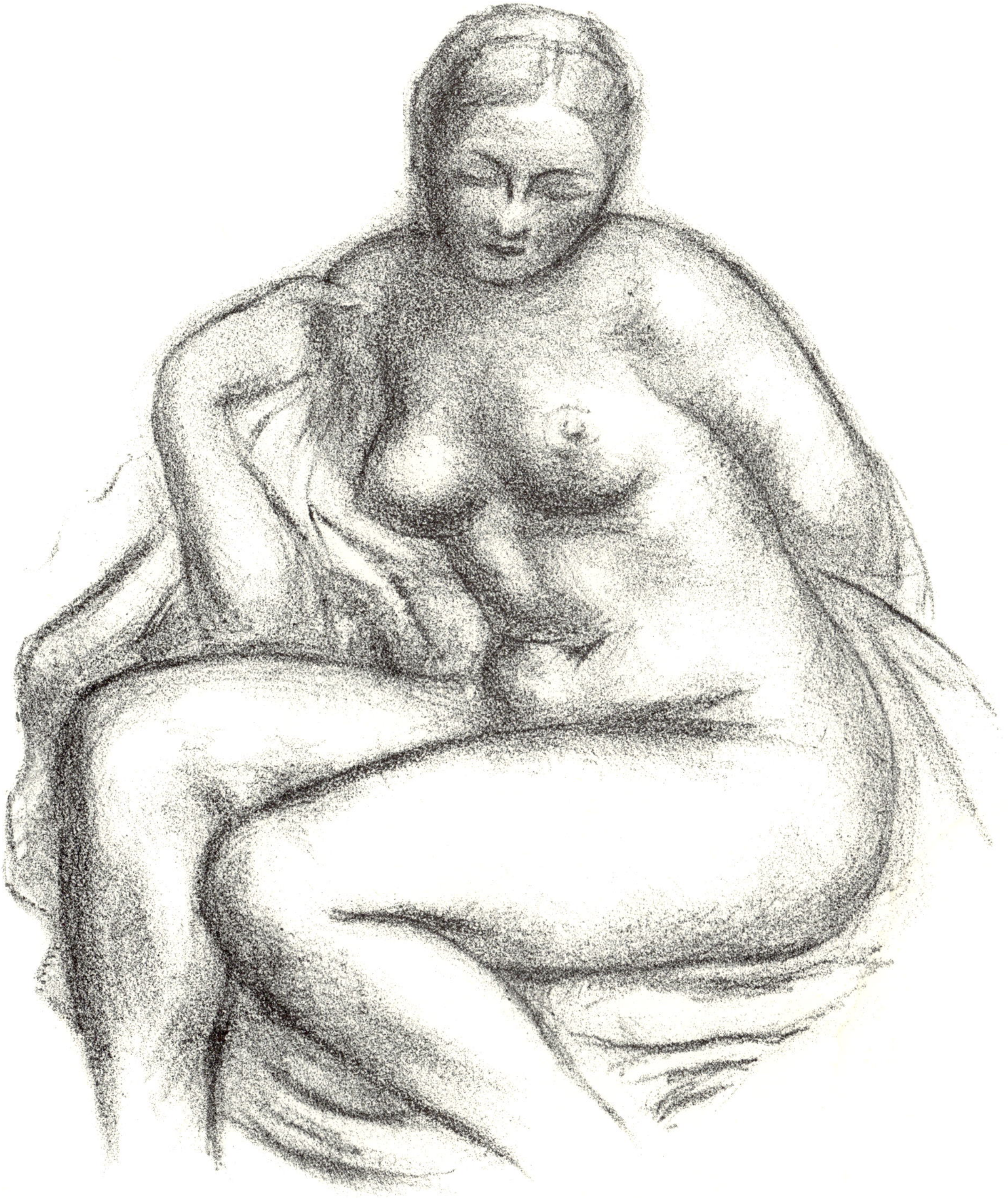

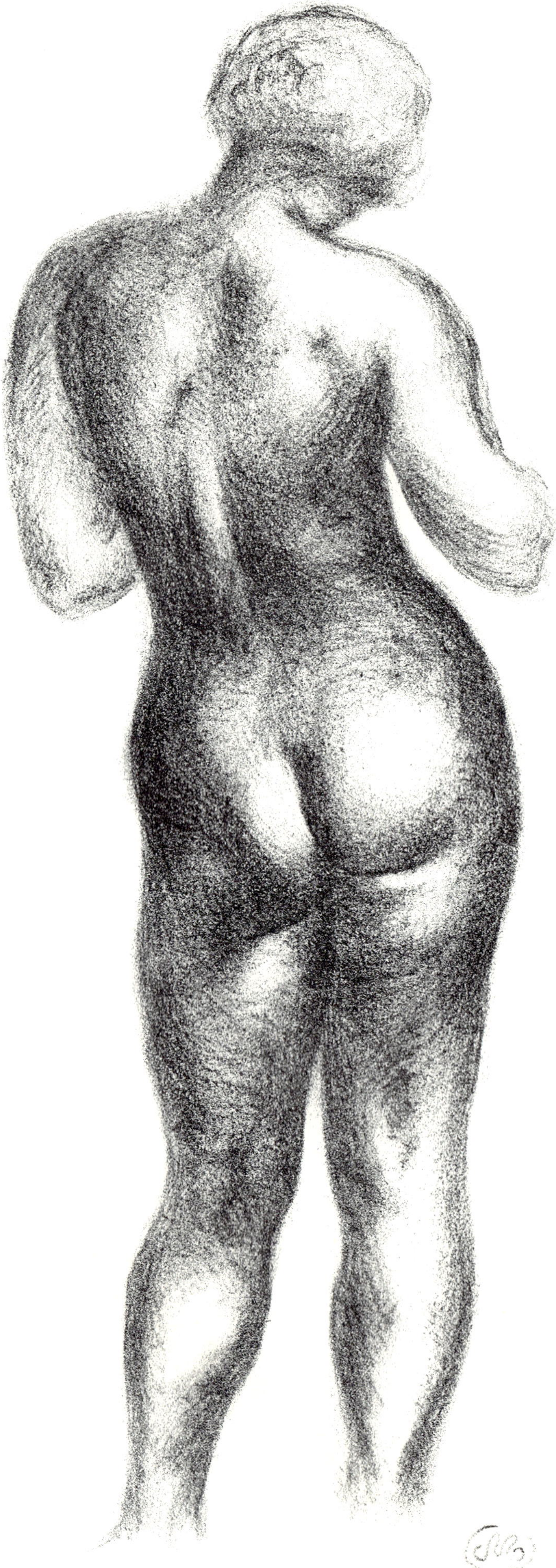

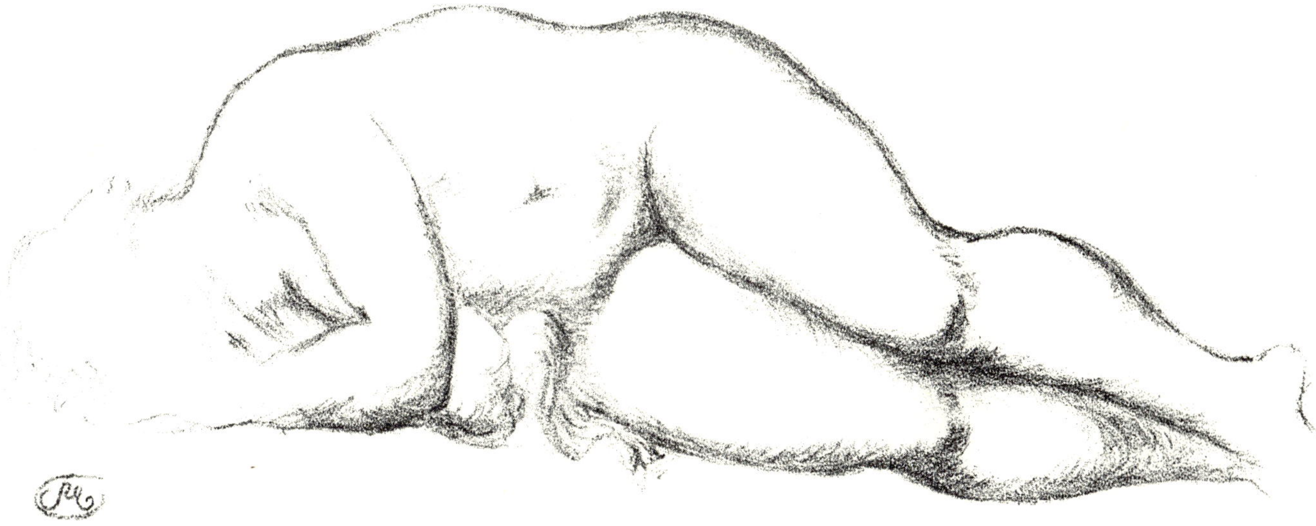

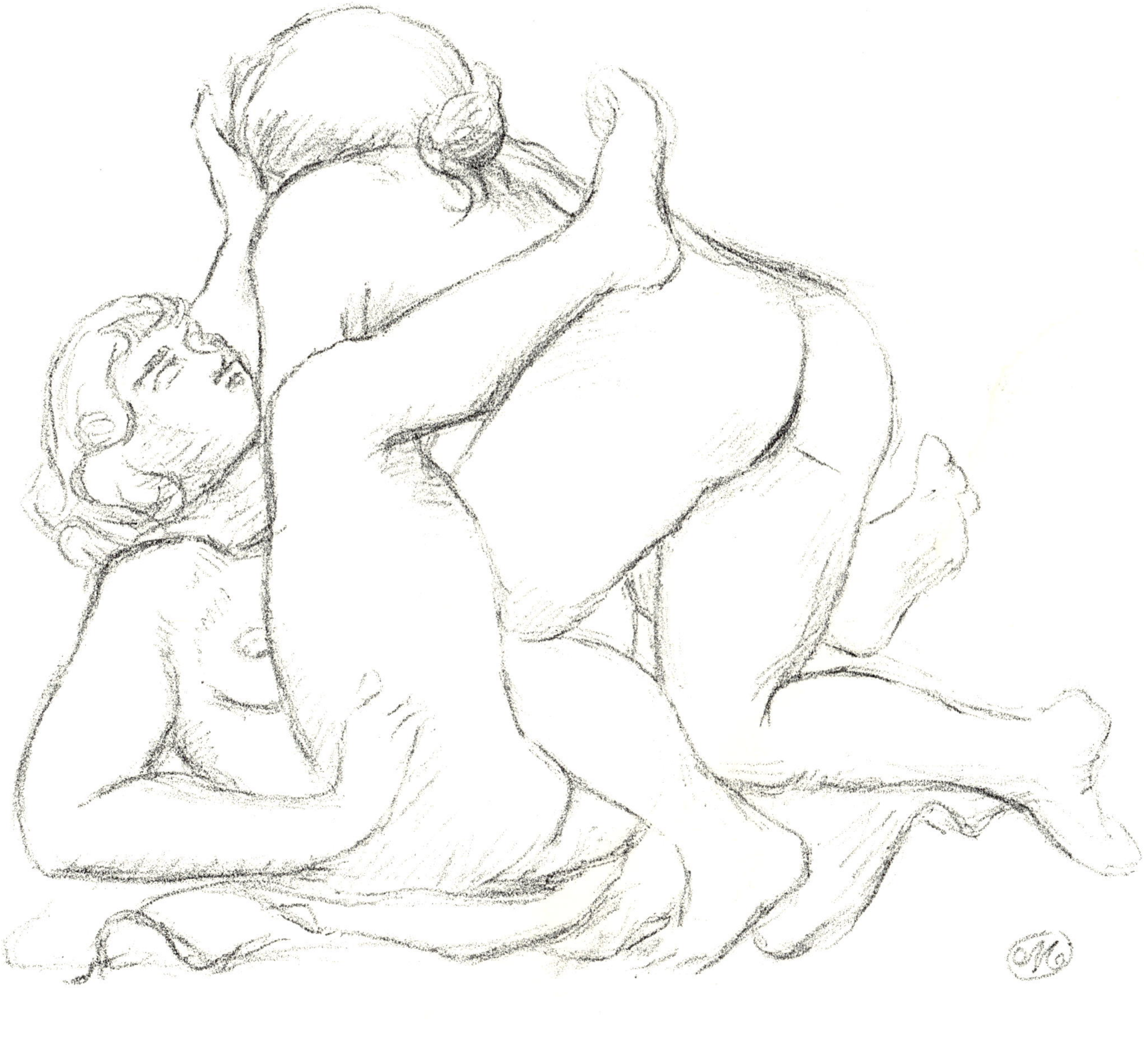

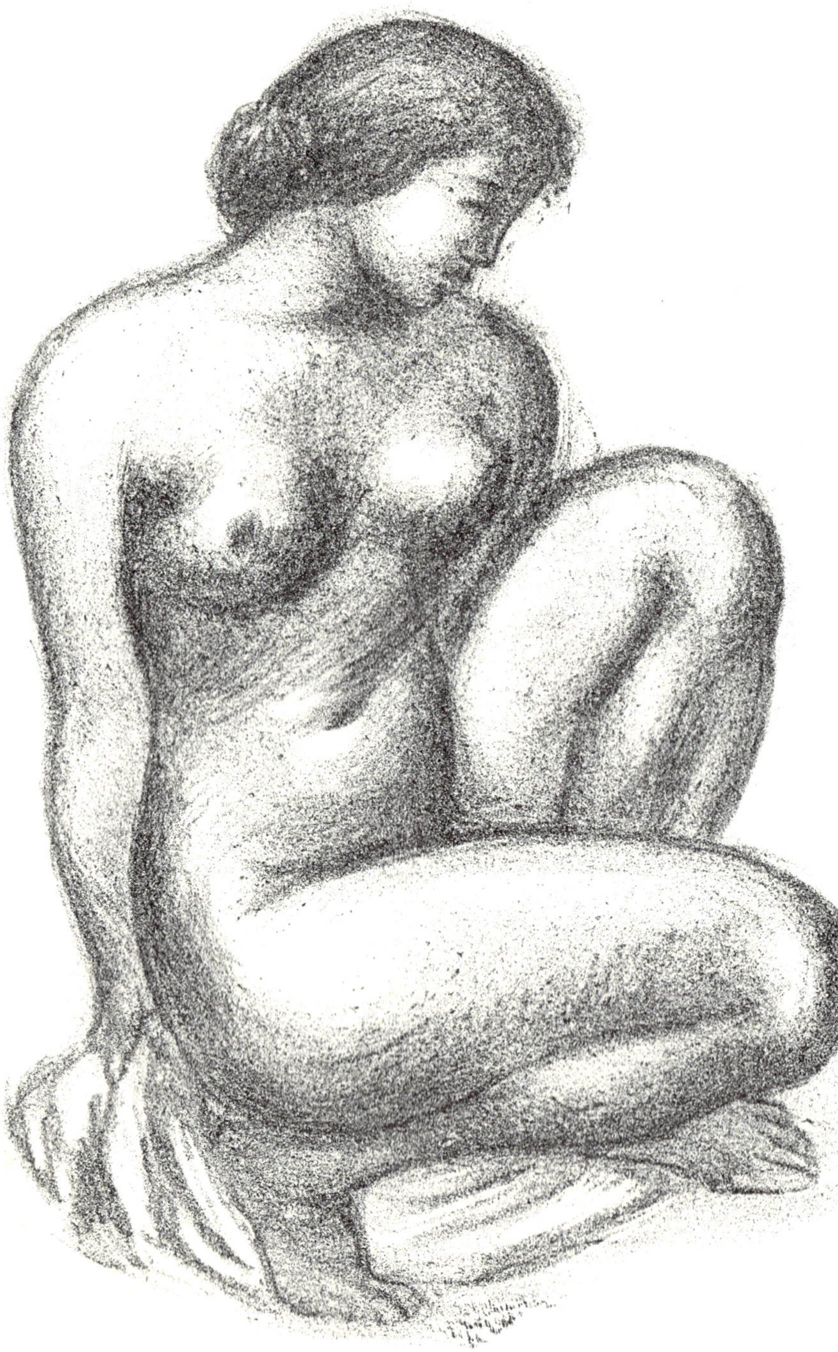

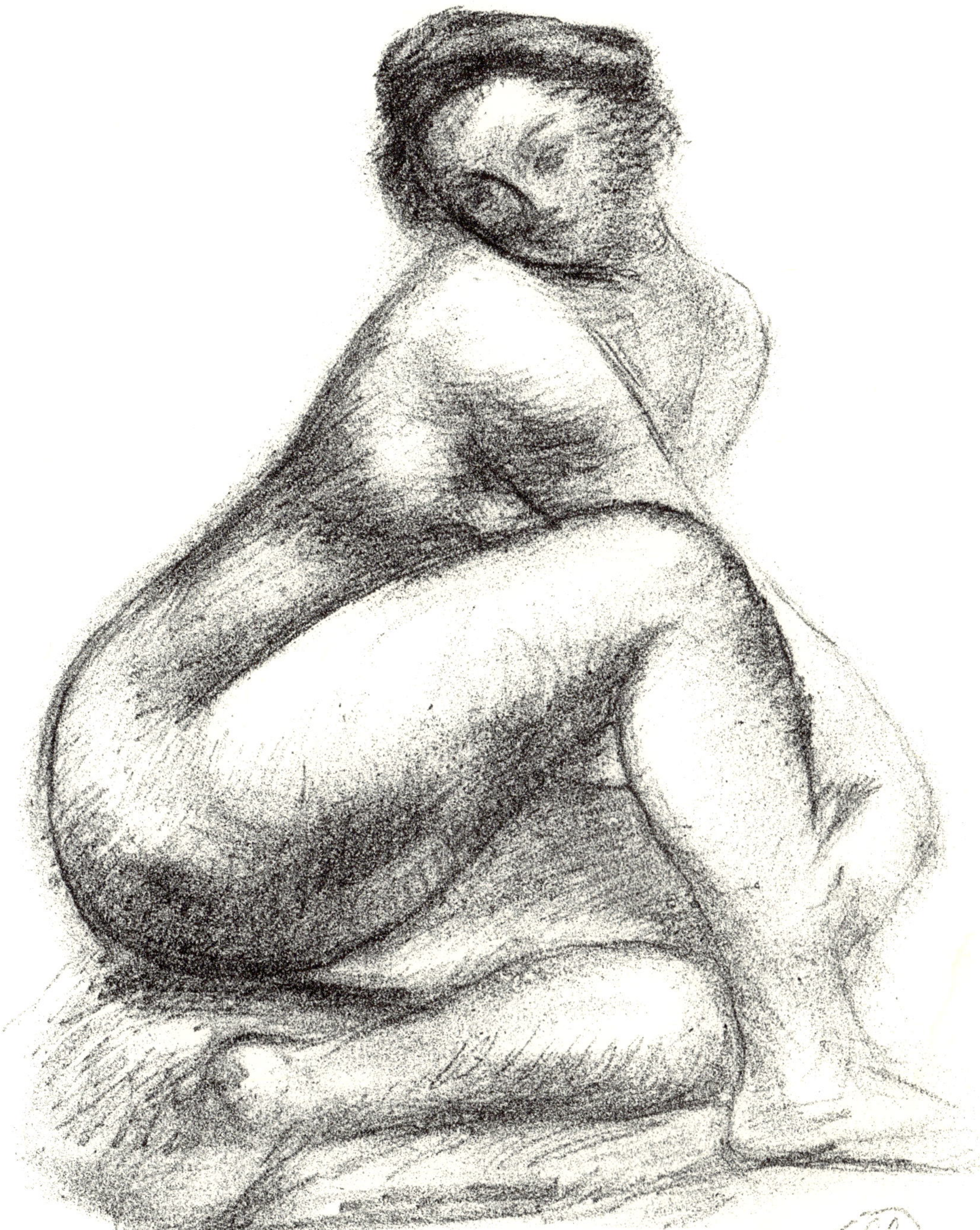

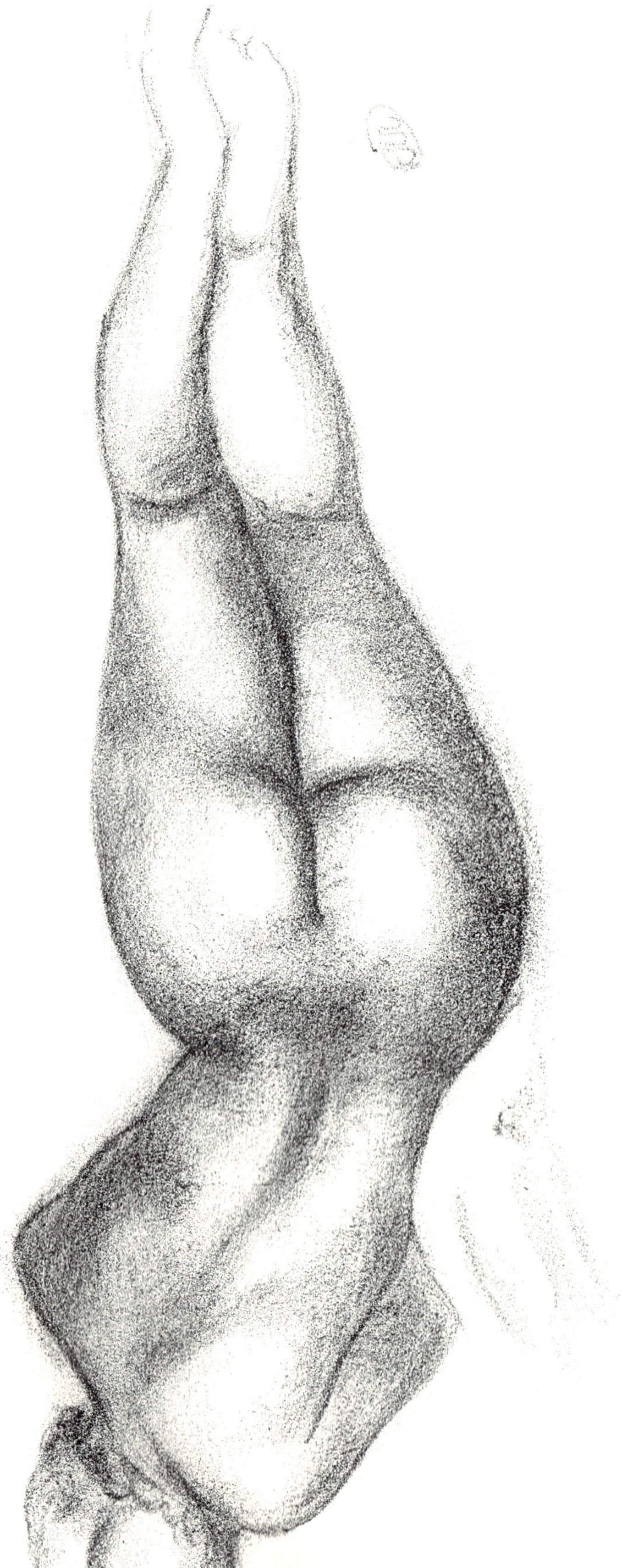

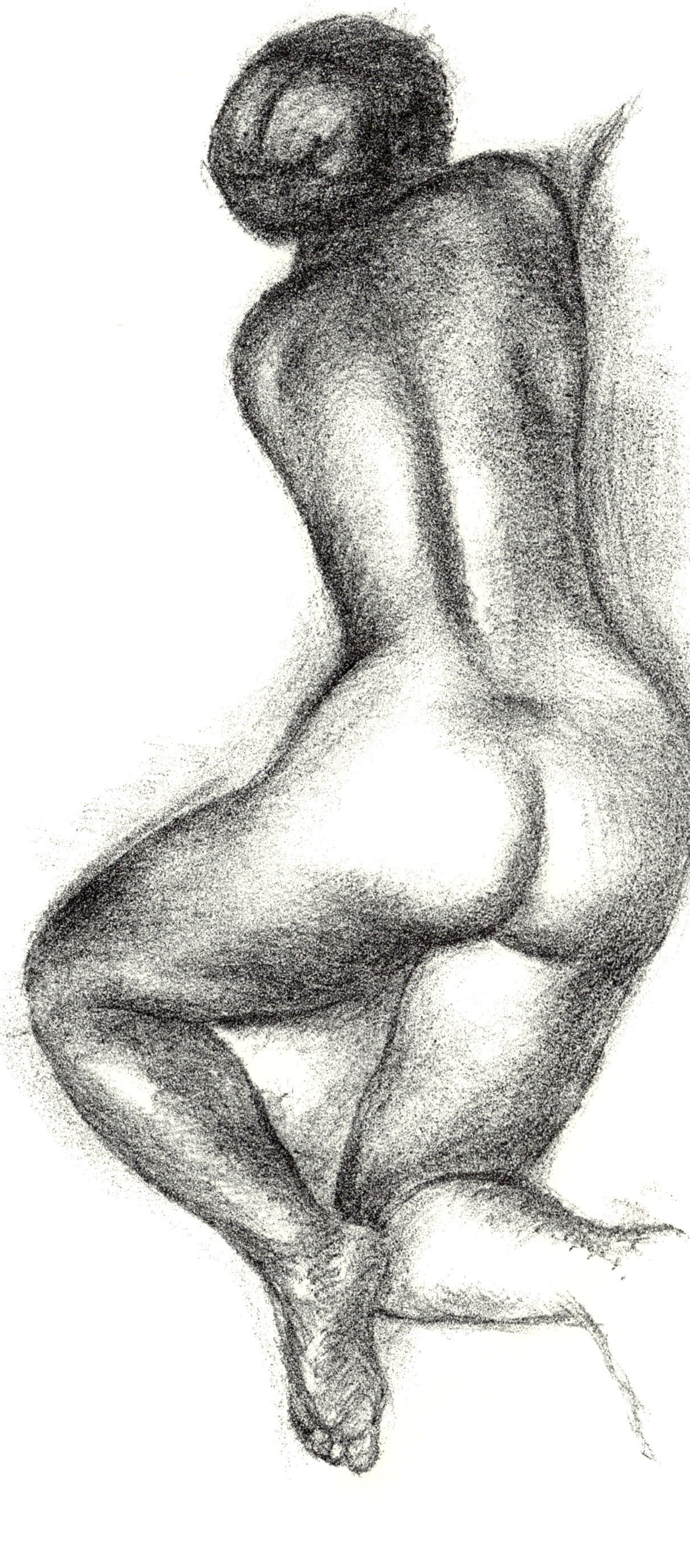

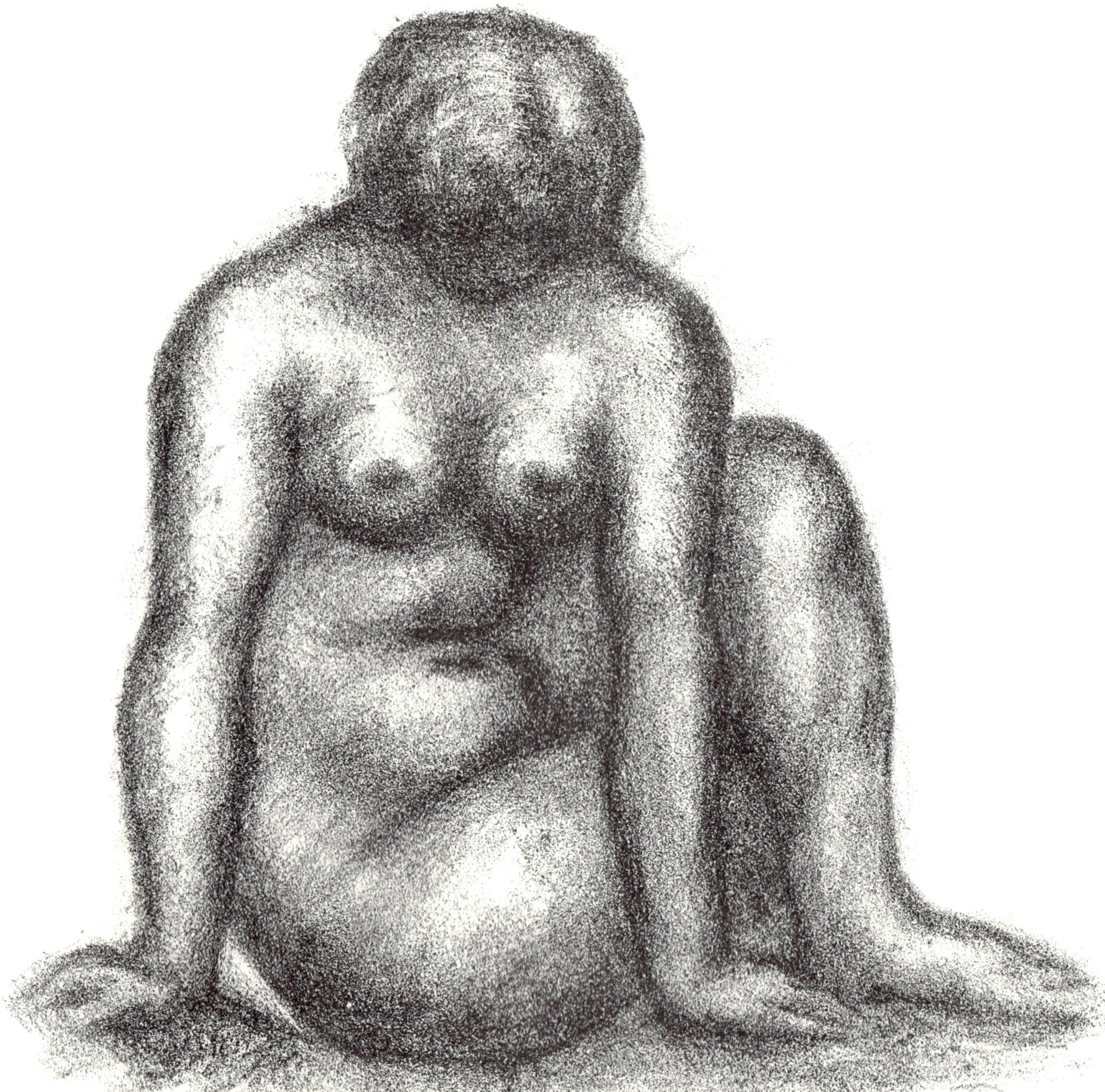

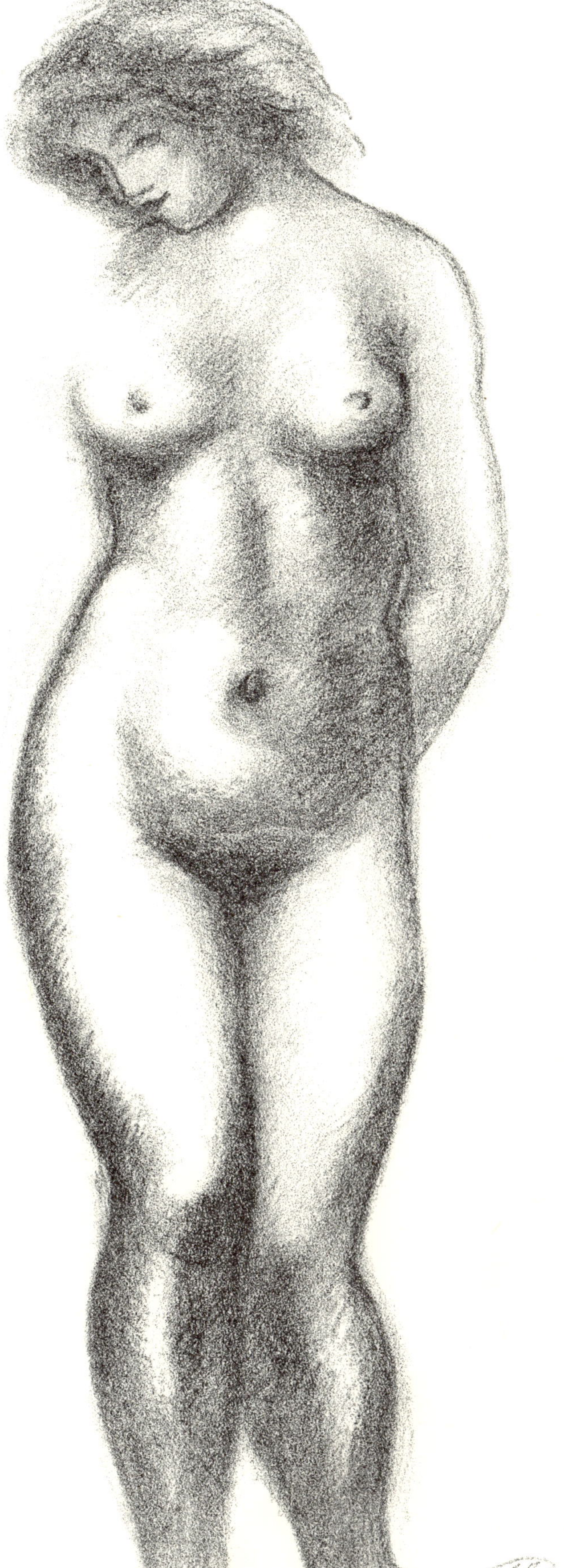

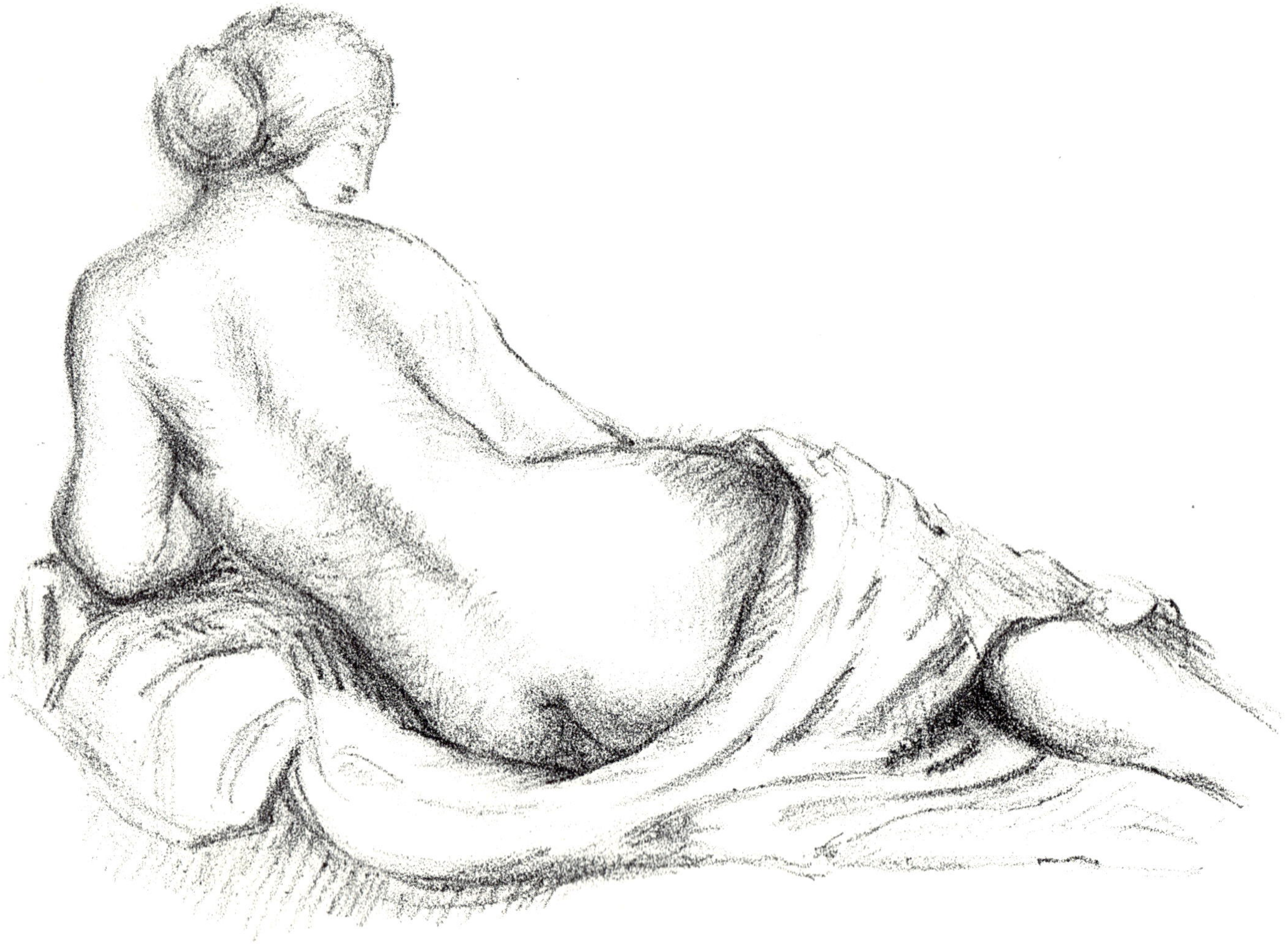

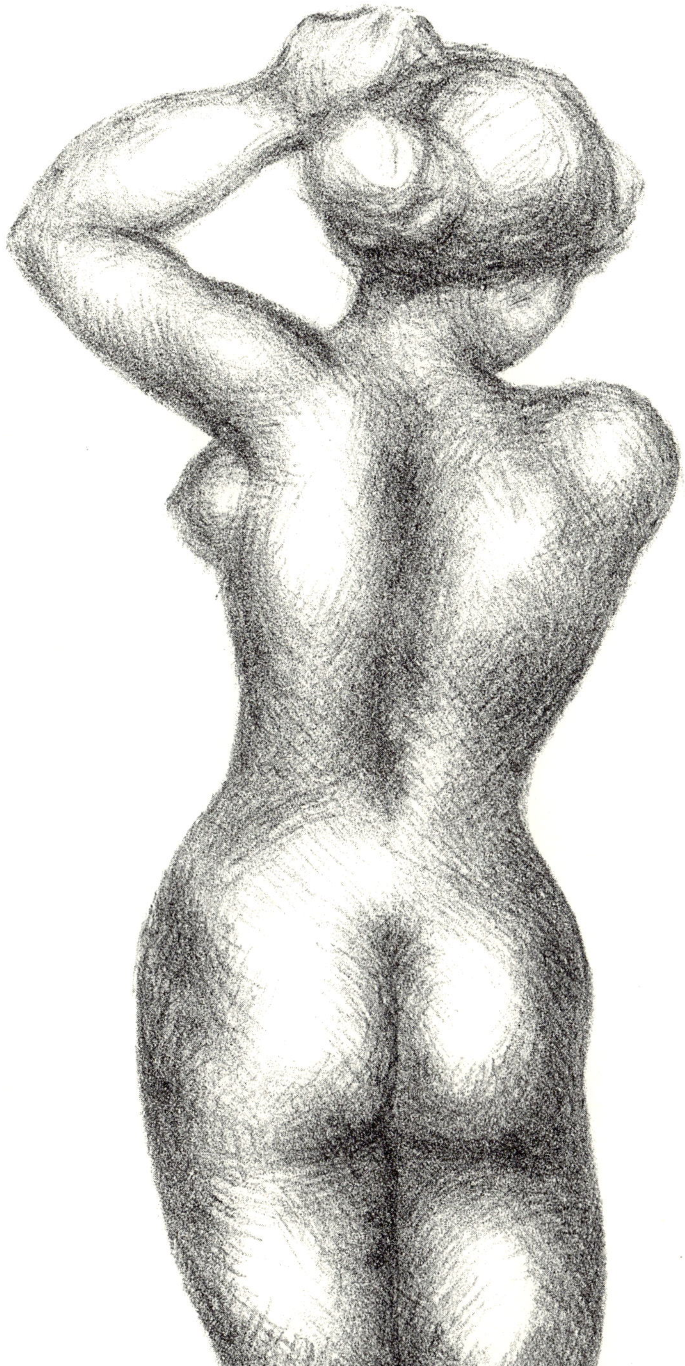

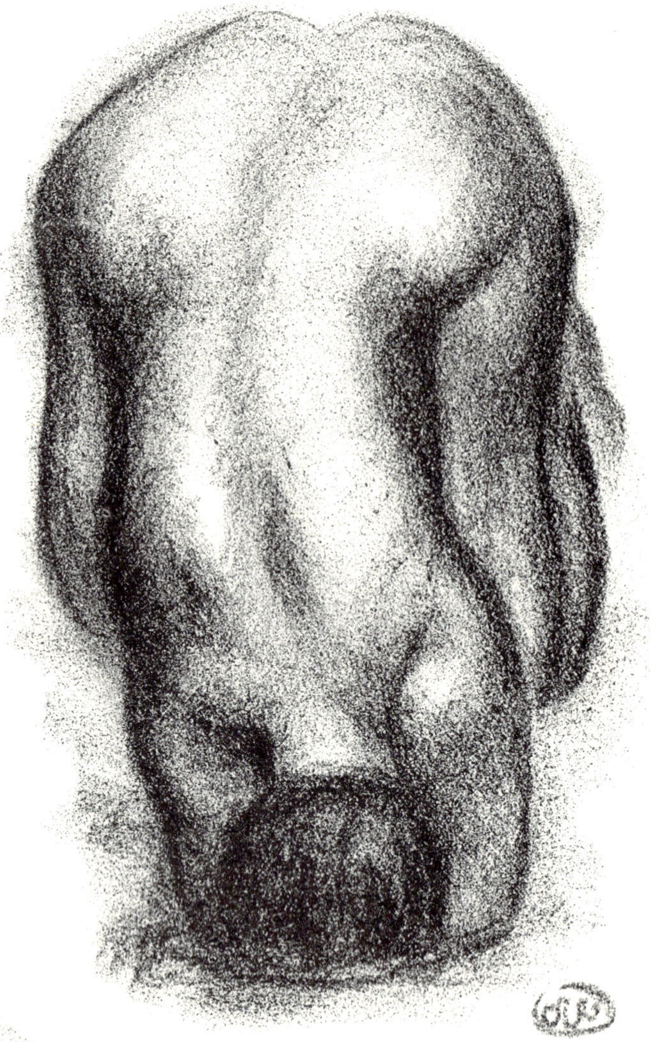

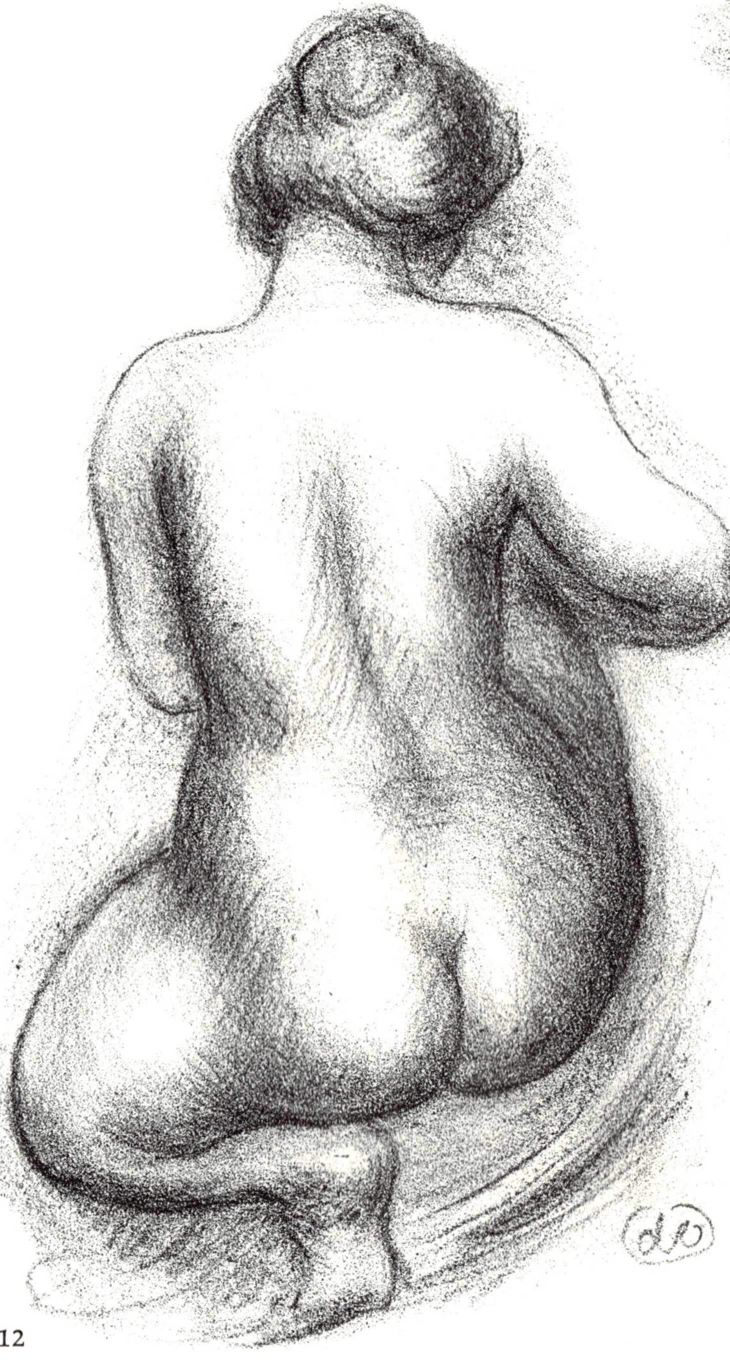

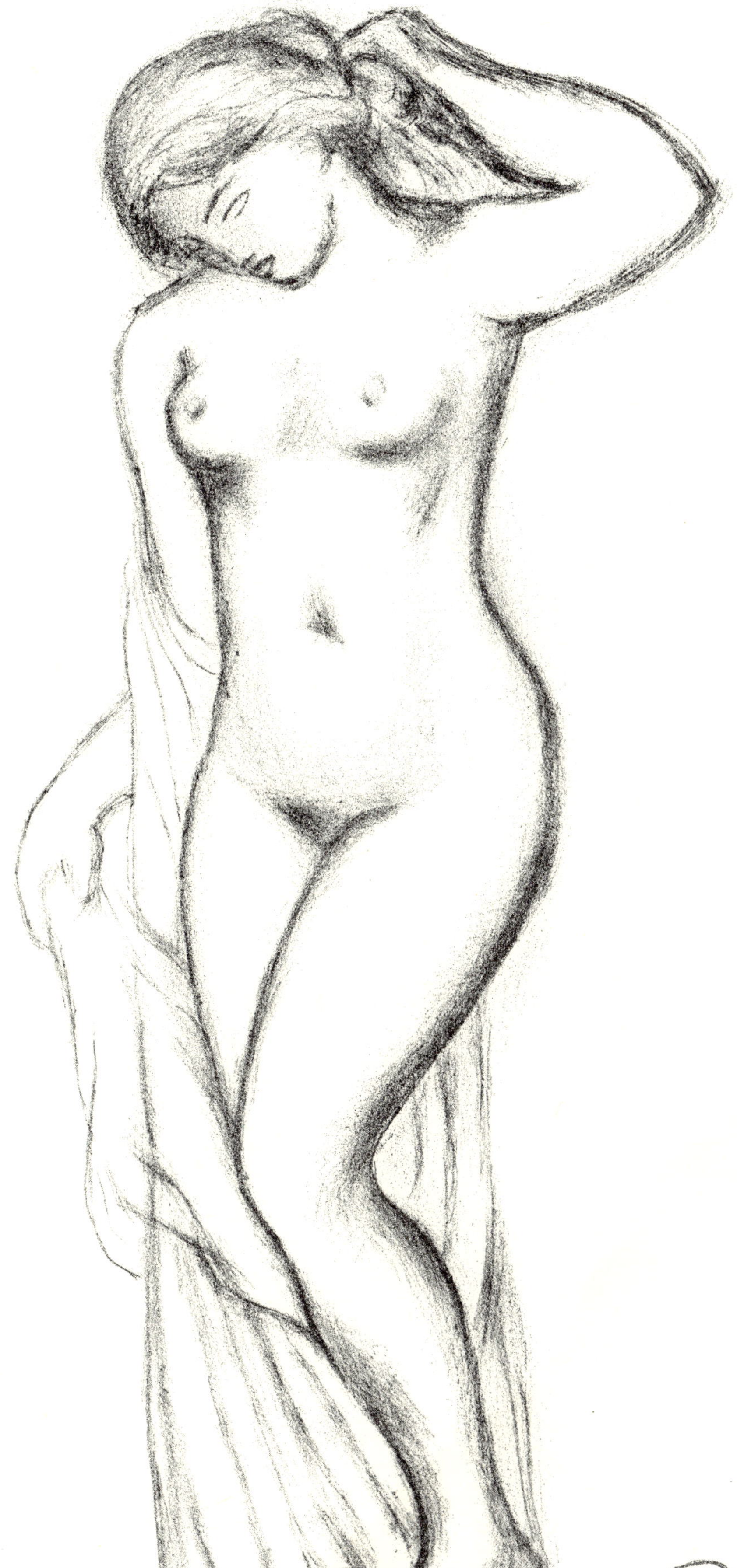

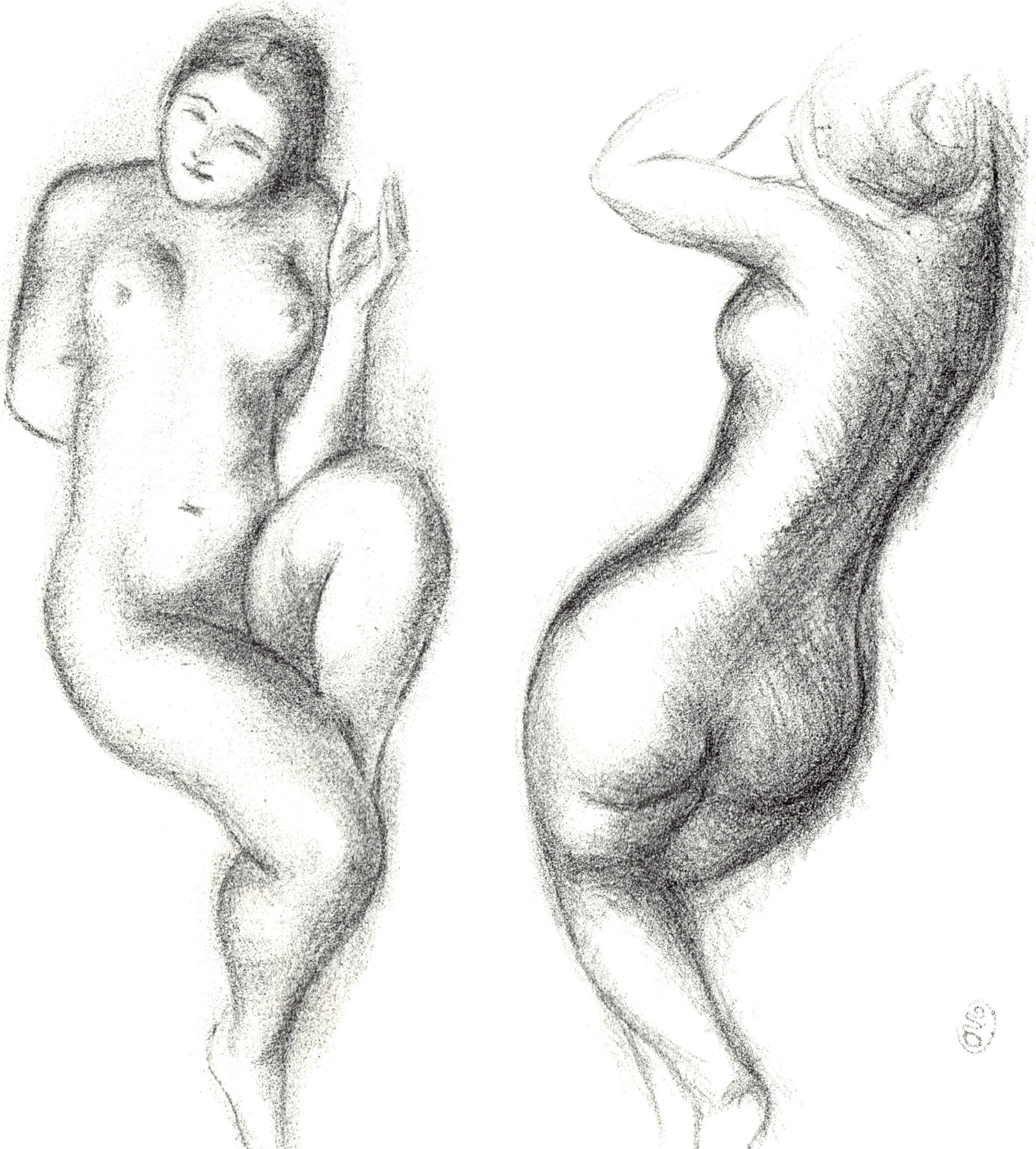

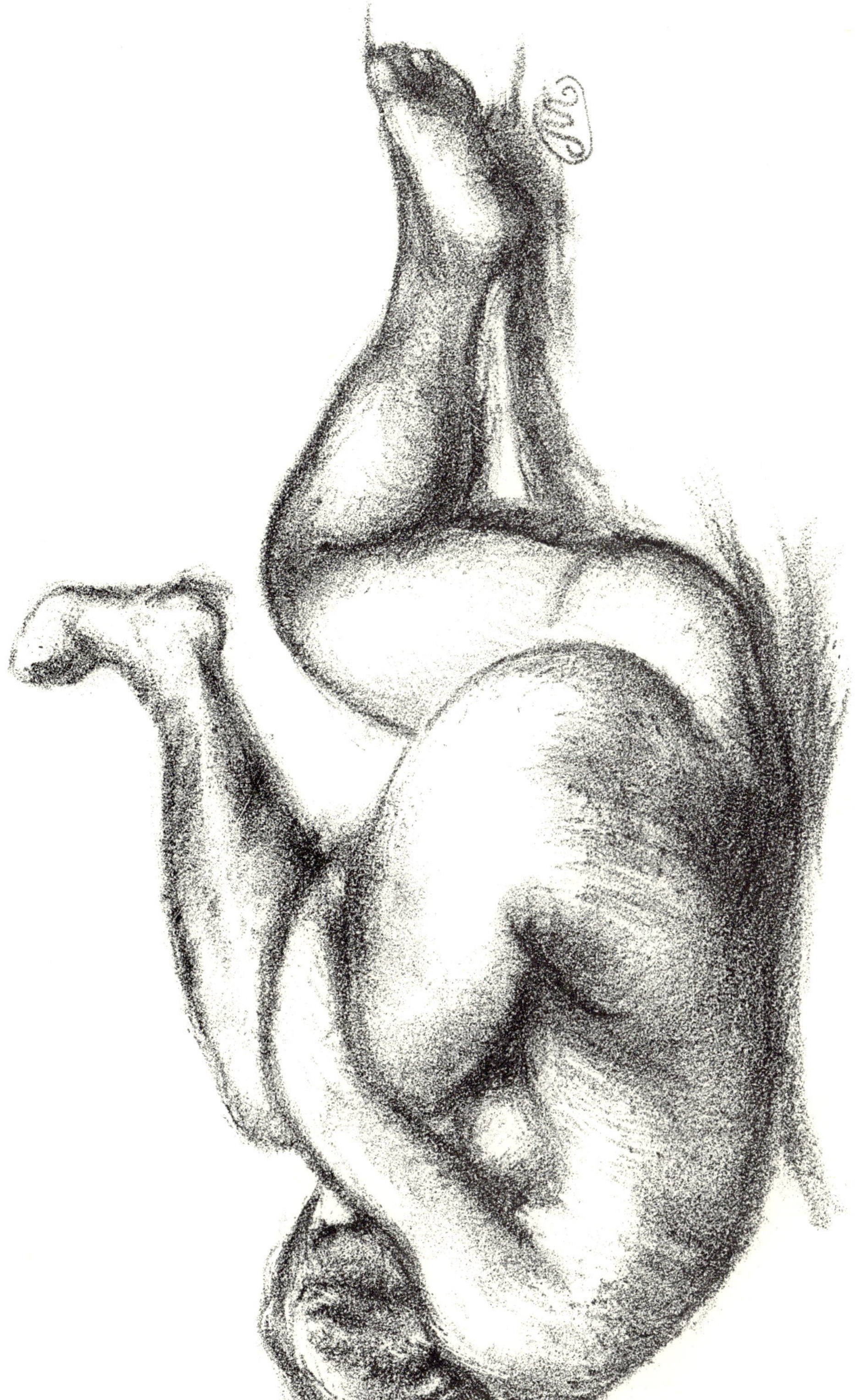

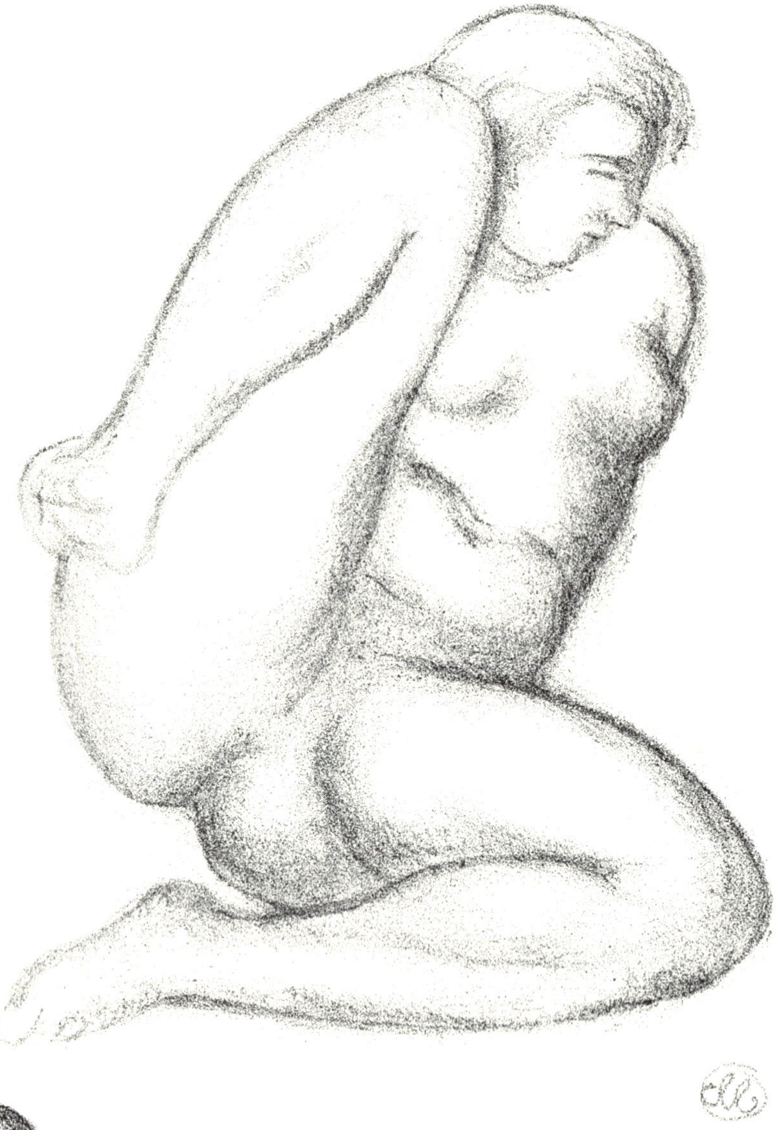

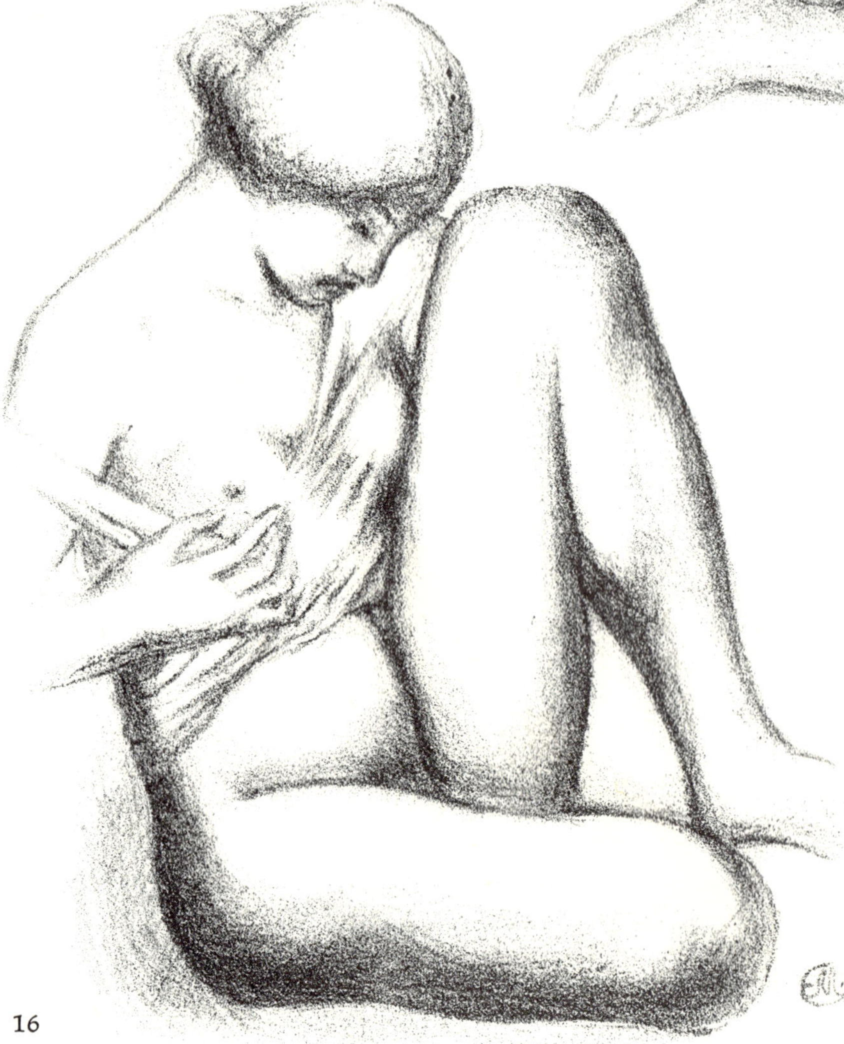

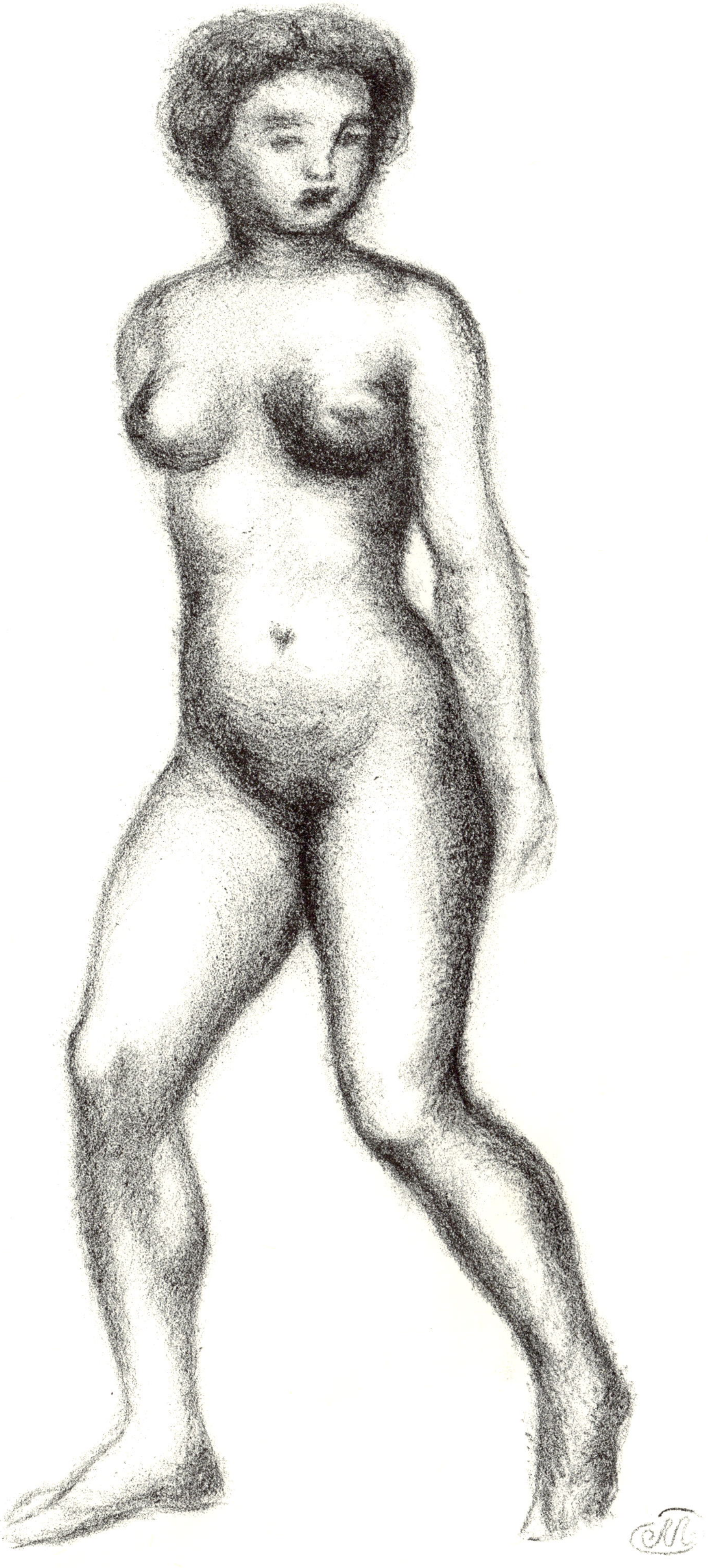

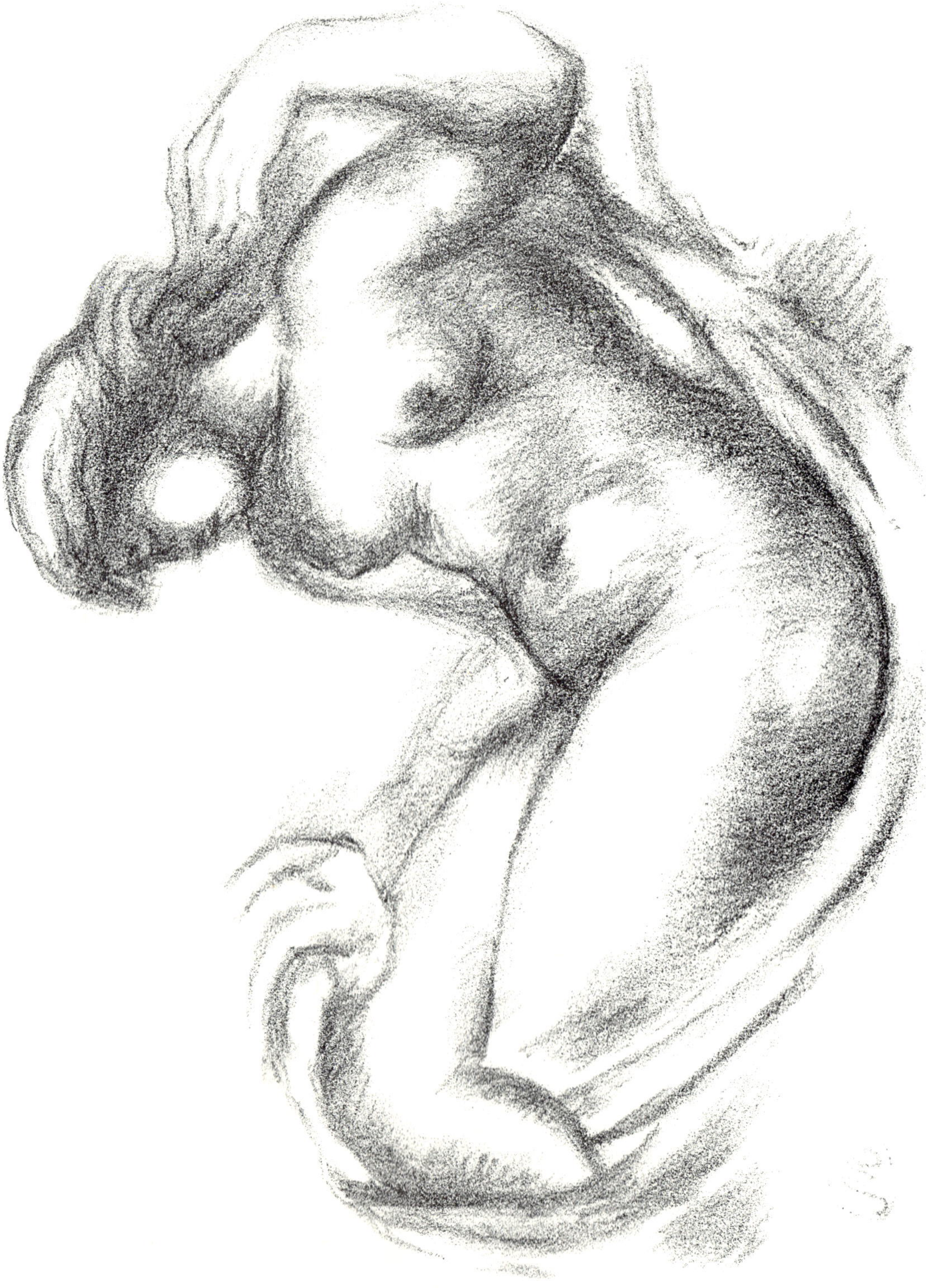

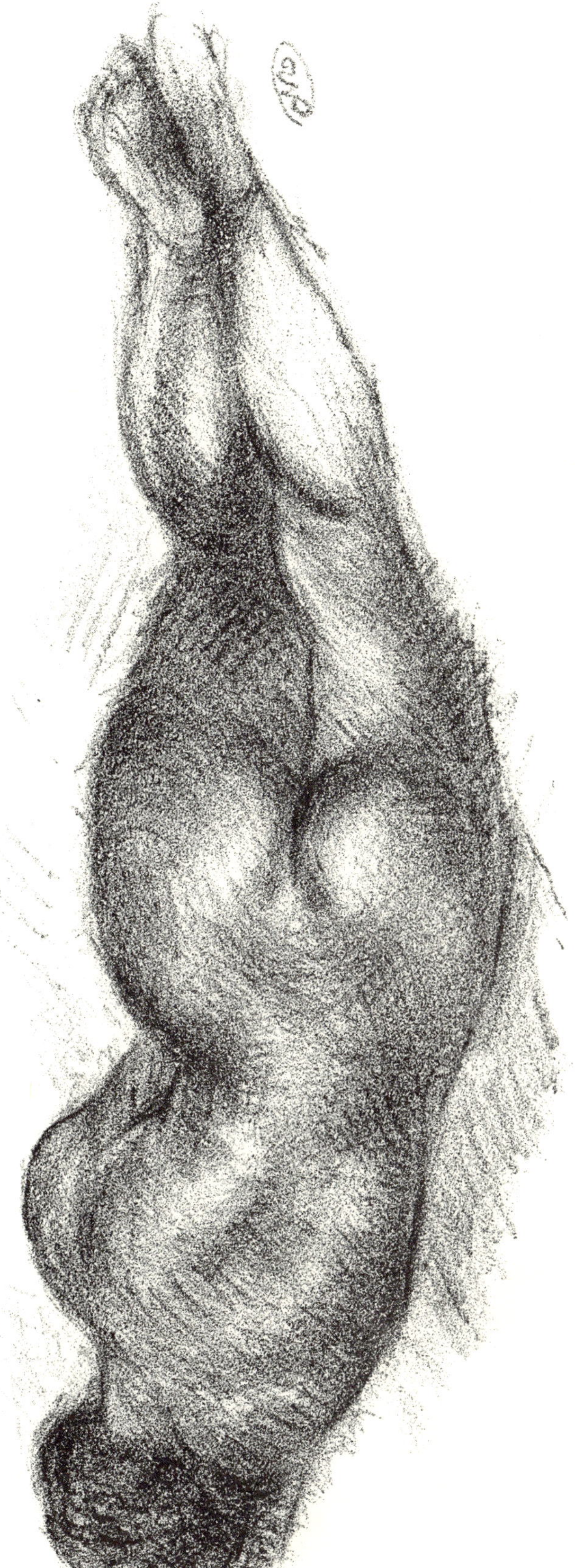

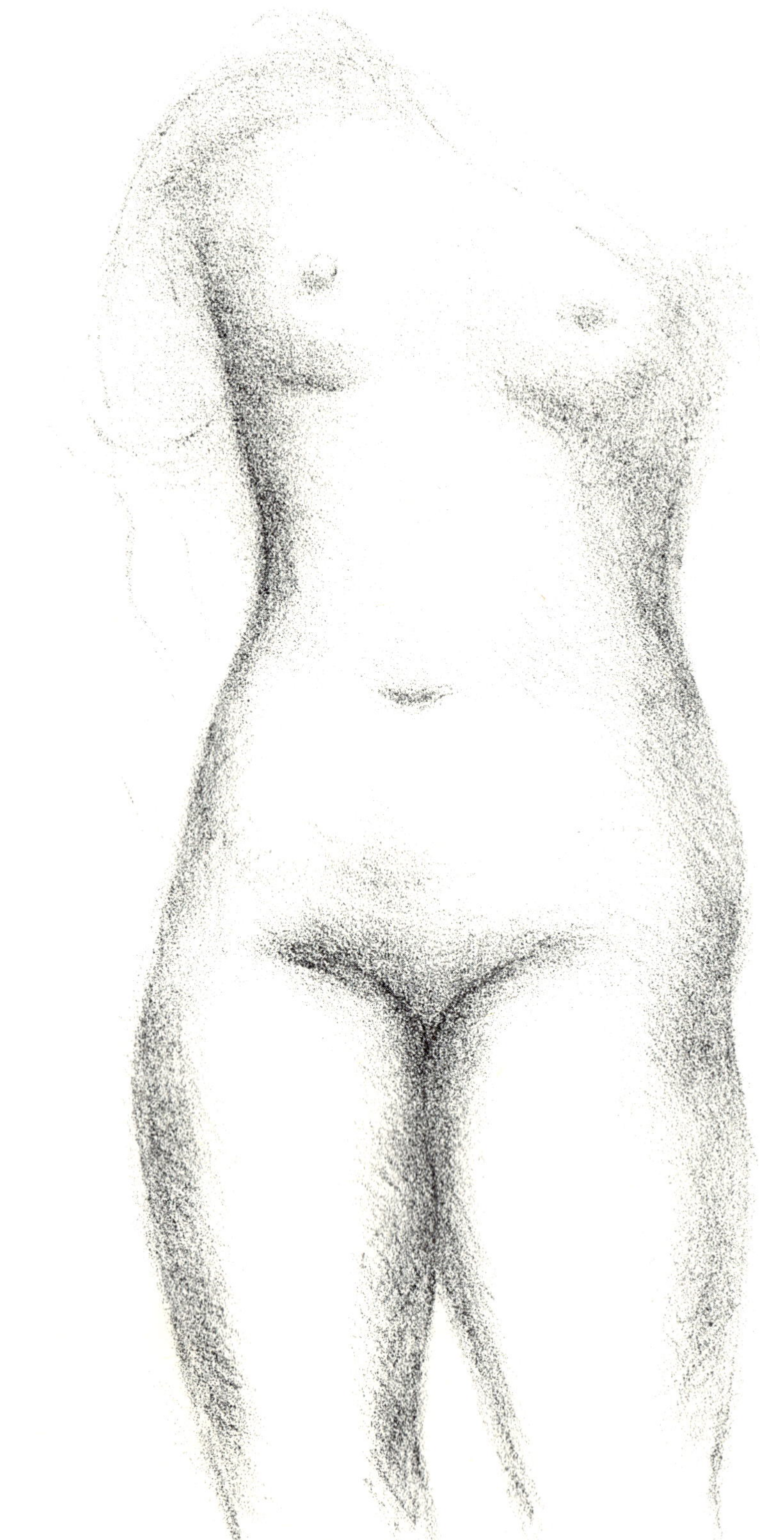

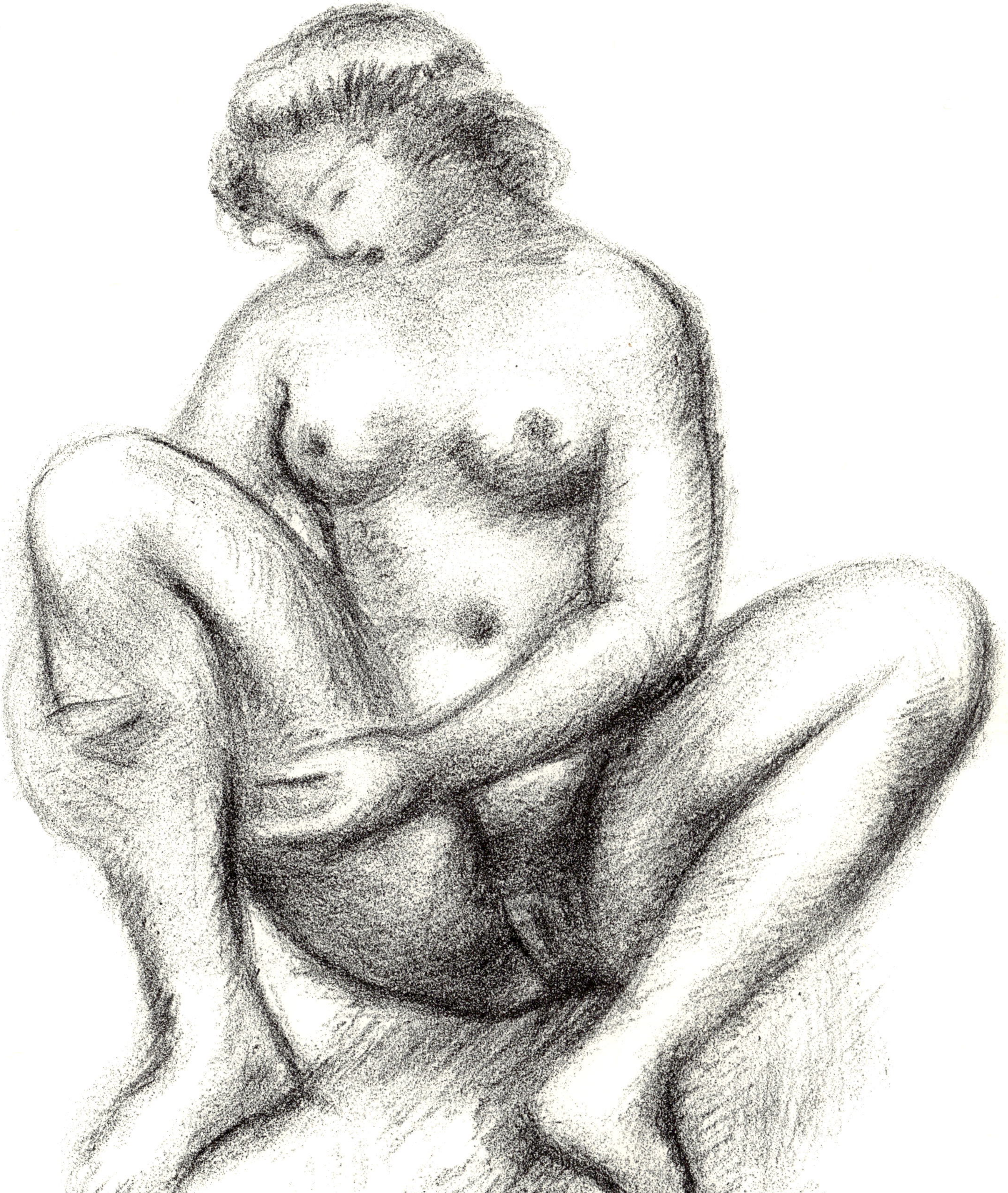

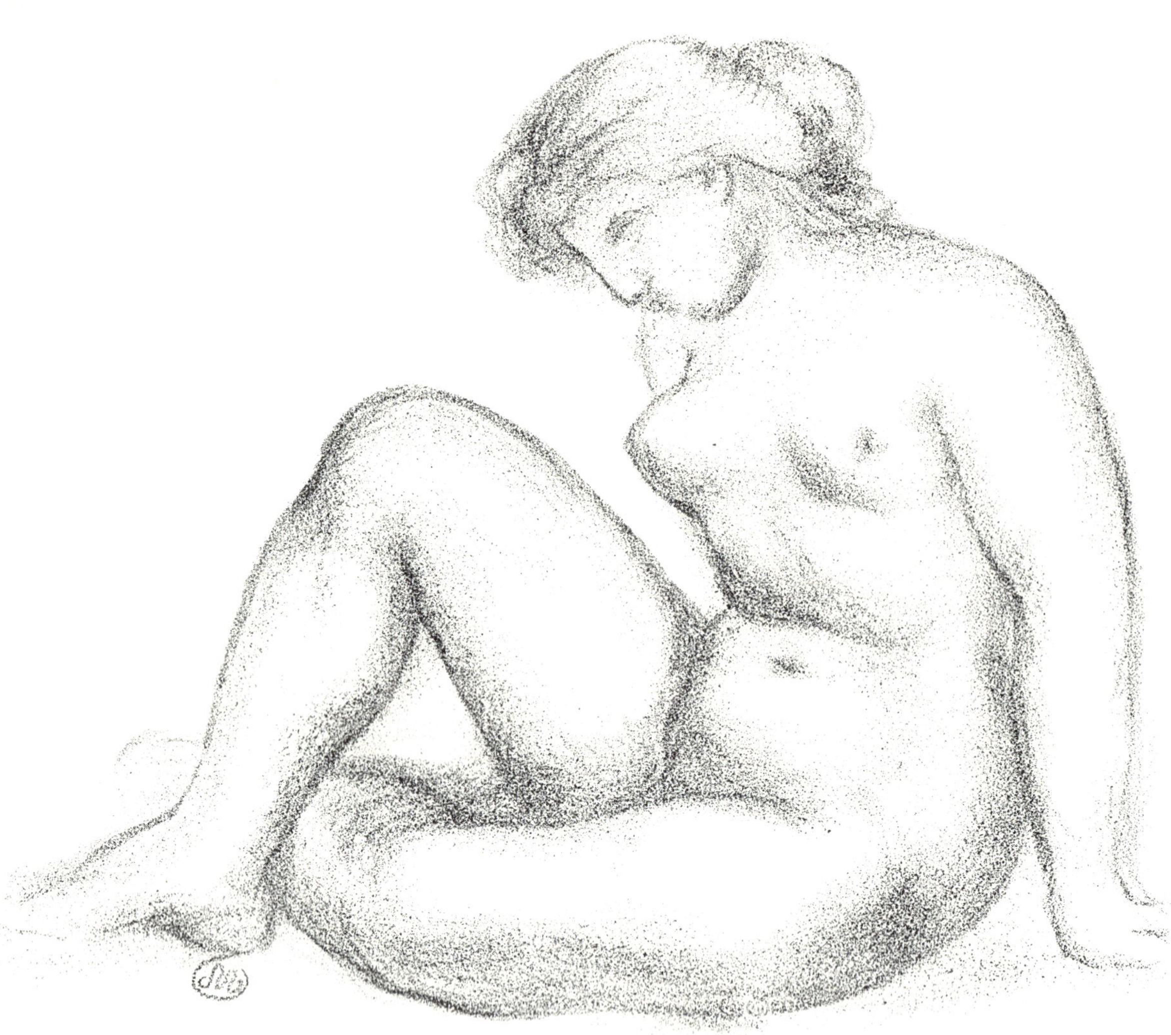

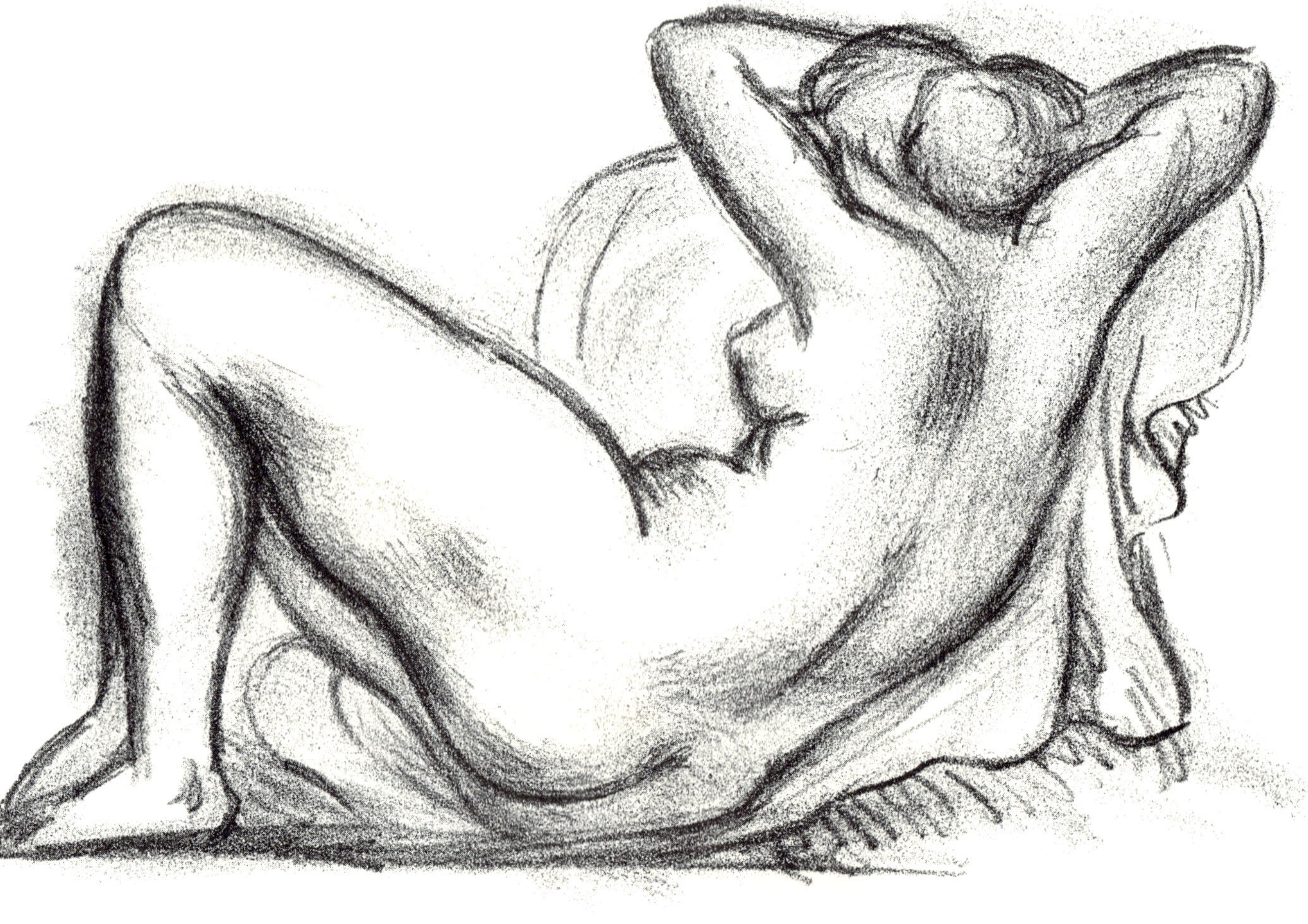

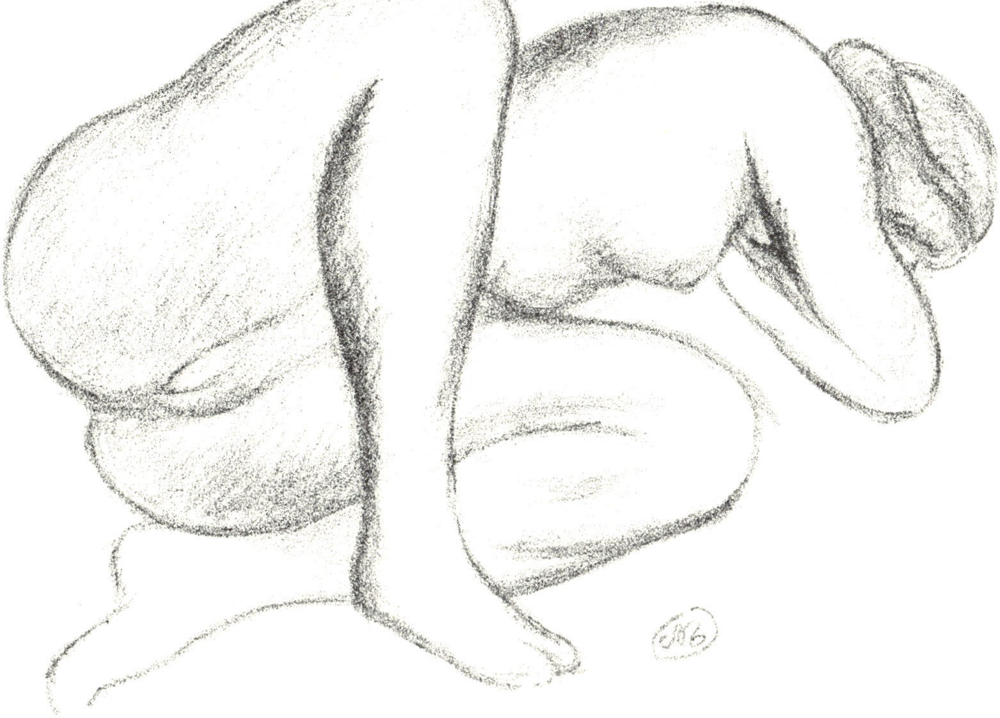

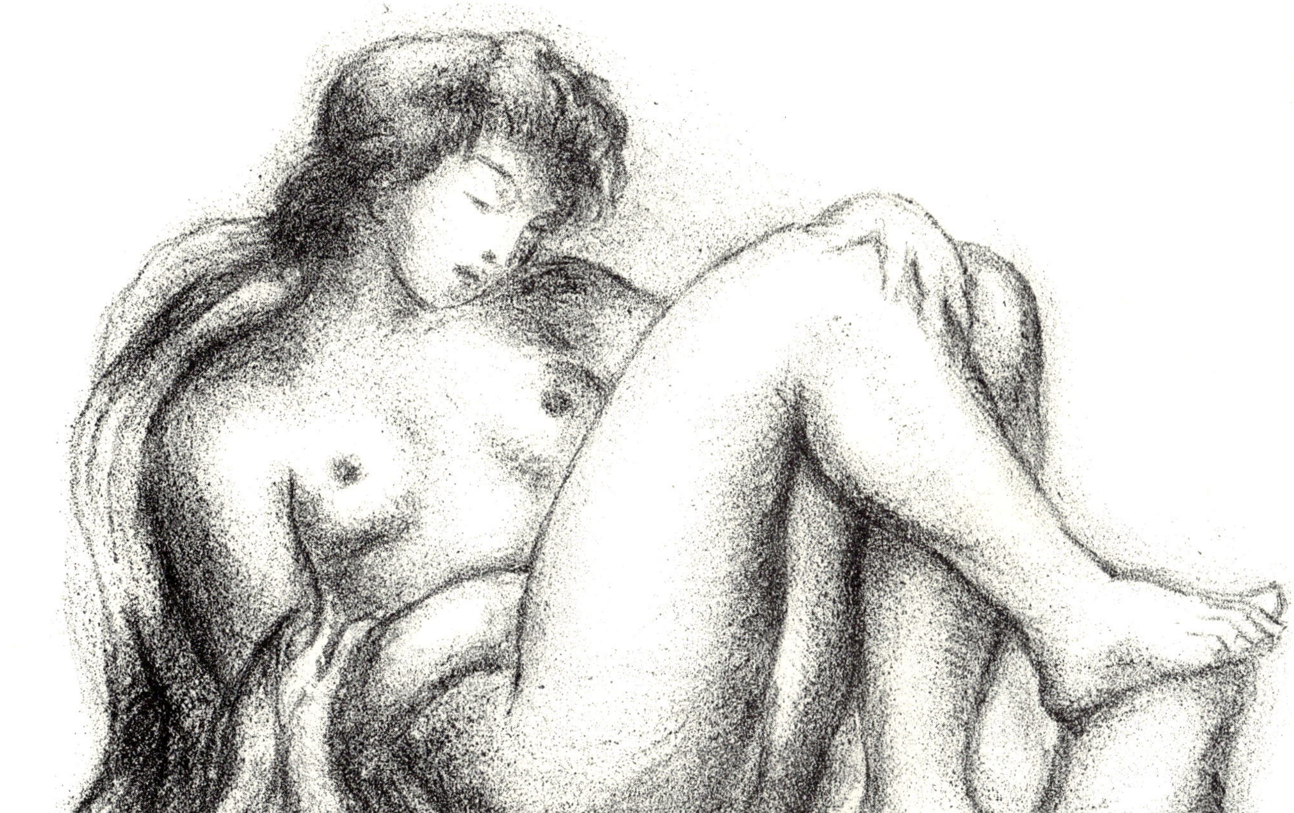

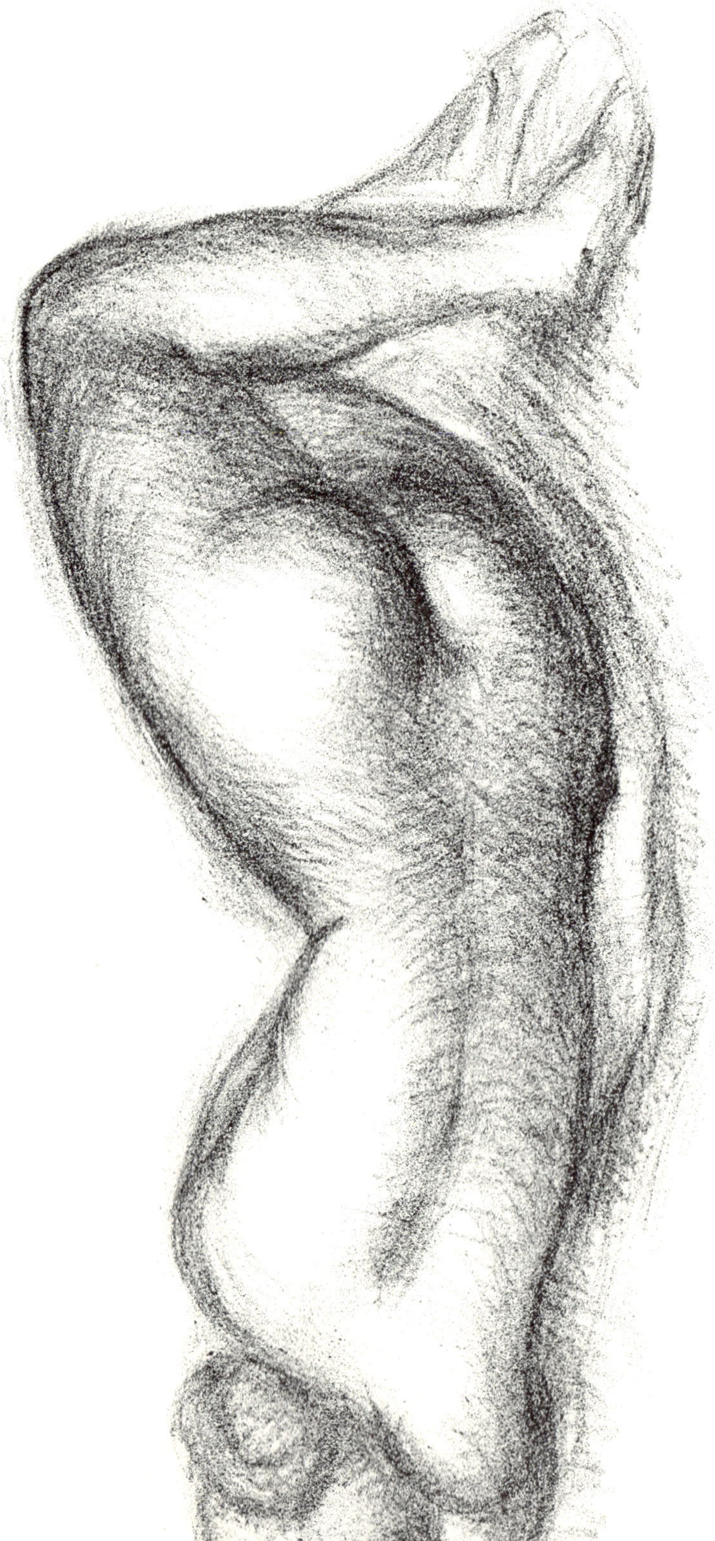

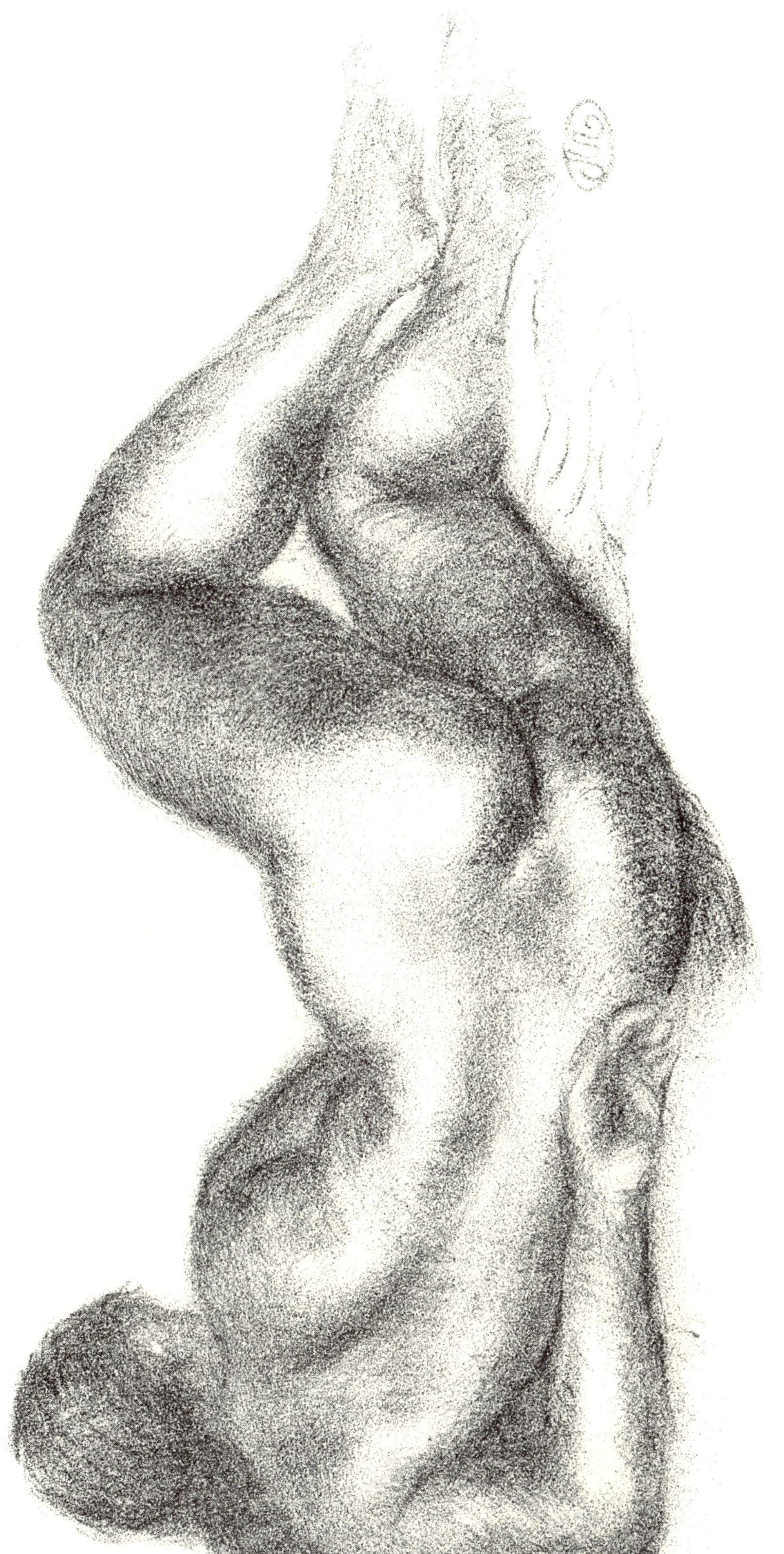

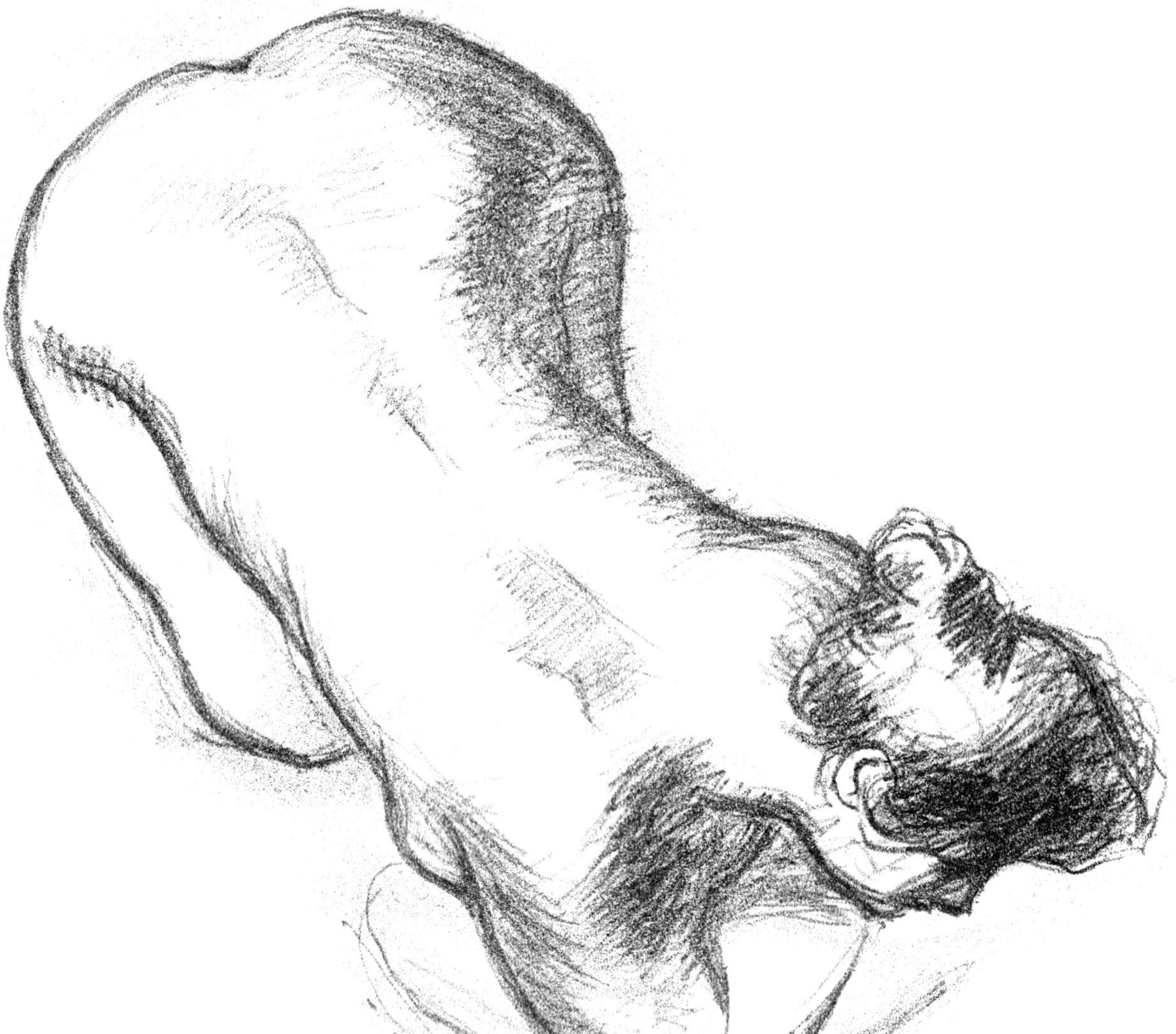

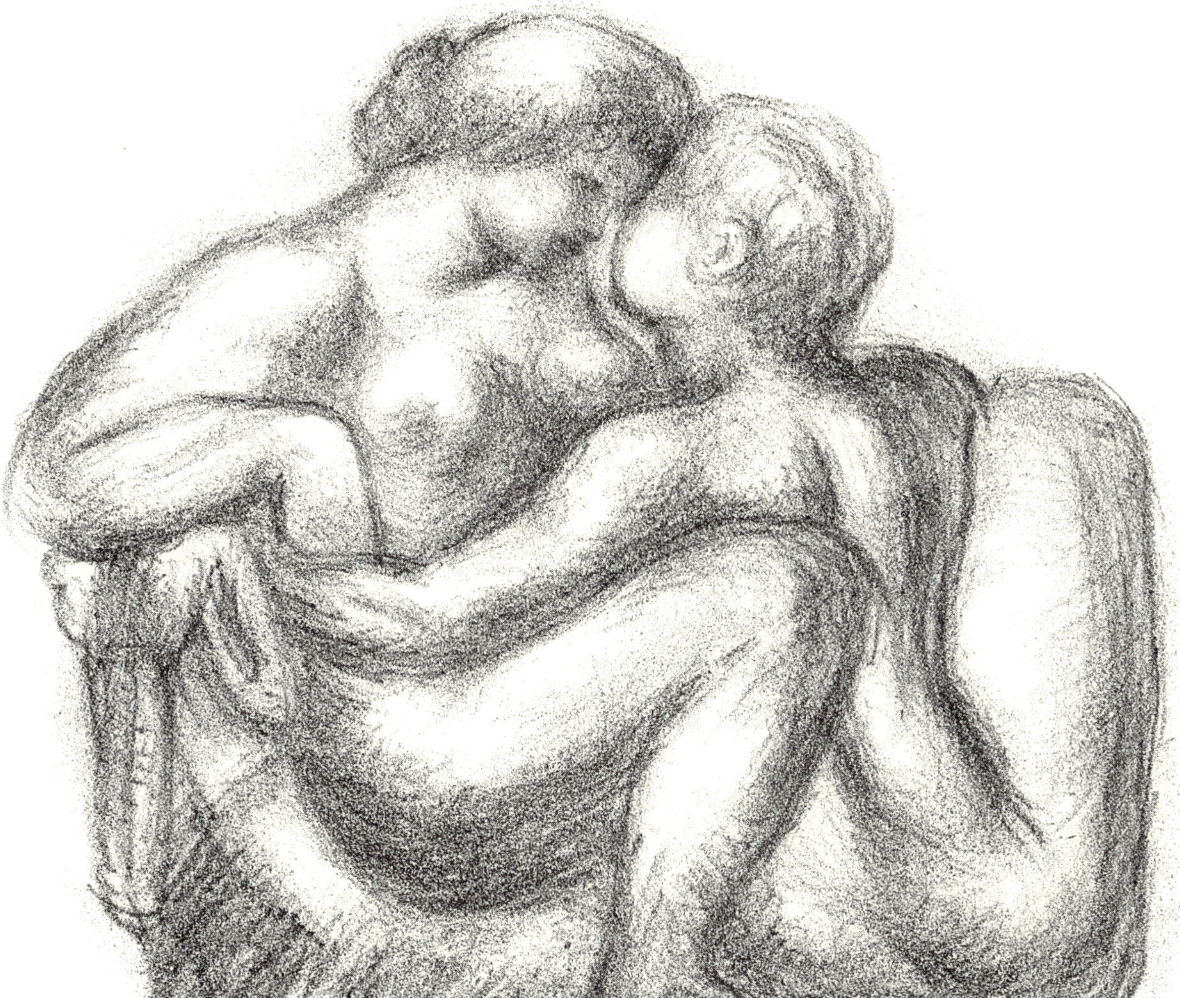

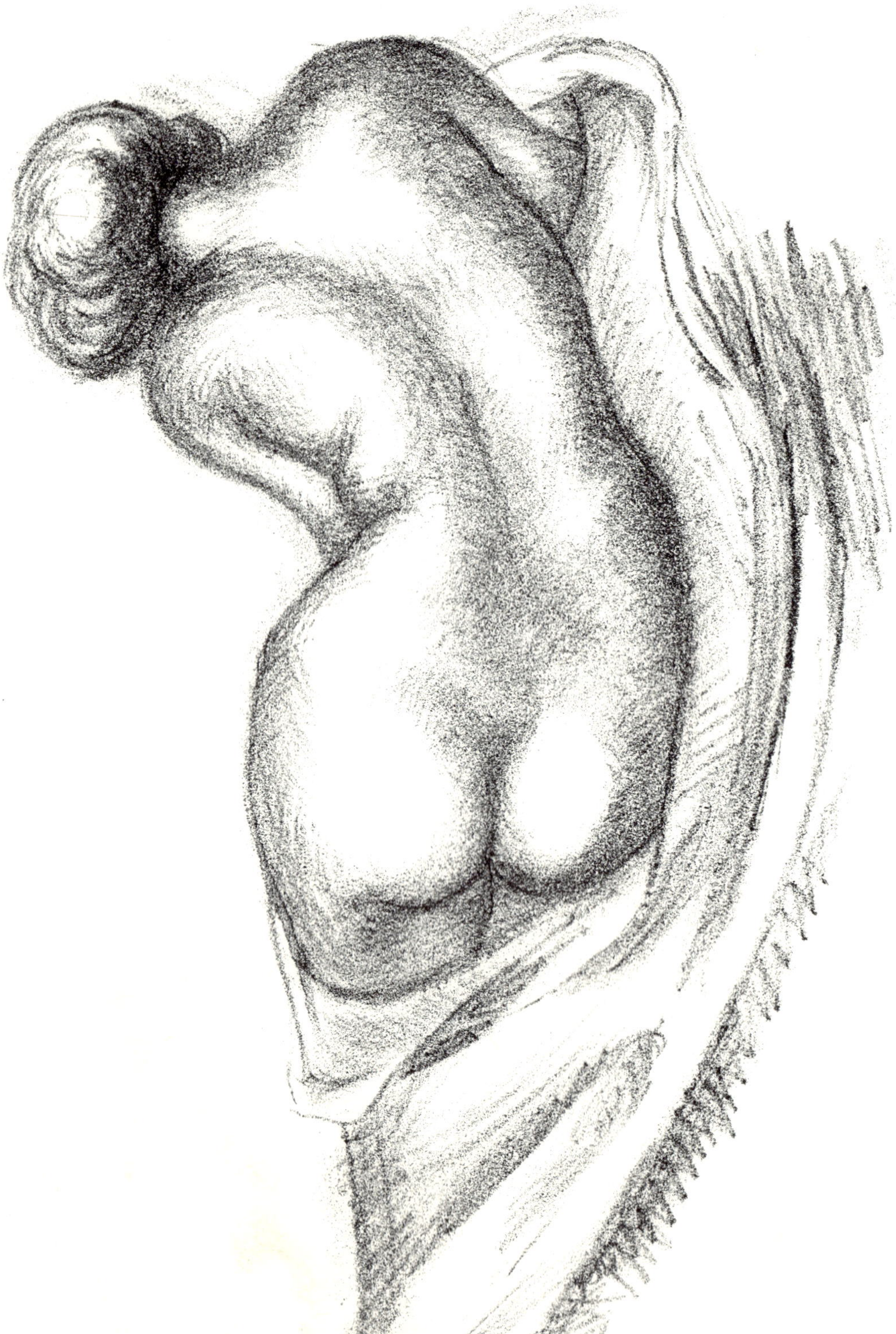